Mastering CryENGINE

Use CryENGINE at a professional level and master the engine's advanced features to build AAA quality games

Sascha Gundlach

Michelle K. Martin

PUBLISHING

BIRMINGHAM - MUMBAI

Mastering CryENGINE

First published: April 2014

Production Reference: 1040414

Published by Packt Publishing Ltd.

Livery Place
35 Livery Street
Birmingham B3 2PB, UK.

ISBN 978-1-78355-025-8

www.packtpub.com

Cover Image by Berker Siino (berkersiino@gmail.com)

Credits

Authors

Sascha Gundlach

Michelle K. Martin

Reviewers

Hendrik Polczynski

Ross Rothenstine

Sheetanshu

Acquisition Editor

Owen Roberts

Content Development Editor

Neeshma Ramakrishnan

Technical Editors

Pragnesh Bilimoria

Pooja Nair

Nikhil Potdukhe

Copy Editors

Alisha Aranha

Roshni Banerjee

Gladson Monteiro

Adithi Shetty

Project Coordinator

Priyanka Goel

Proofreaders

Simran Bhogal

Maria Gould

Ameesha Green

Paul Hindle

Indexers

Mariammal Chettiyar

Monica Ajmera Mehta

Graphics

Ronak Dhruv

Disha Haria

Yuvraj Mannari

Abhinash Sahu

Production Coordinator

Adonia Jones

Cover Work

Adonia Jones

Shantanu Zagade

About the Authors

Sascha Gundlach has been working in the games industry for over a decade and started his career as a script programmer in a small game studio in the early 2000s. He worked for Crytek for eight years, working on games such as *Crysis*, *Crysis: Warhead*, and *Crysis 2*.

He is a CryENGINE expert and has provided countless training sessions and individual training to CryENGINE licensees in the past years.

In 2013, he founded his own game development company, MetalPop Games, together with his partner and Crytek veteran Michelle K. Martin in Orlando, Florida.

He spends his days working on video game projects and provides consulting work for other game projects.

Michelle K. Martin is a software engineer in the game industry, specializing in animation systems. She started her career with the German developer, Crytek, working on projects such as *Crysis* and *Crysis 2*. During her career, Michelle has helped develop and improve CryENGINE's animation system with several features. Being an expert in CryENGINE, she has provided a lot of support and training to CryENGINE licensees over the years, helping their team to get the most out of the engine.

In 2013, she founded MetalPop Games together with her partner and Crytek veteran Sascha Gundlach. It is an indie game development studio and they are currently working on their first title.

When she's not in front of the computer programming, she is most likely to be in front of the computer playing games.

More about Sascha and Michelle's company MetalPop Games can be found at www.metalpopgames.com.

About the Reviewers

Hendrik Polczynski is a software developer from Germany. He has been working on software development for over 10 years. He likes to take on a variety of fields, from the automation industry to web, UI, and game development. You can find his open source projects on github.com/hendrikp or on his YouTube channel. Hendrik is currently maintaining a handful of open source projects around the CryDev community using CryENGINE 3 FreeSDK. When he is not working, he is working on his Bachelor thesis or helping out in the development of *Miscreated* by Entrada Interactive, which is a post-apocalyptic, survival-based MMORPG; it is unlike anything you've played before.

I would like to thank the following people who have helped me review specific chapters of this book:

Victor Duarte, Simon Hambly, and Chris Ioakeimoglou

Ross Rothenstine has been interested in game development from the instant he sat in front of a computer. Studying all engines, from self-made to commercial, he loves to find ways to tinker with these massive systems and push them to their core, thereafter presenting his findings to universities and teaching courses wherever he may. Game development may be an intimidating task, but with books like these, he's sure you can do it!

Sheetanshu is a professional developer who resides in the metro city of Gurgaon, India. He is currently working to obtain an Engineering degree at the Guru Gobind Singh Indraprastha University. He fell in love with programming during his childhood and since then there was no turning back. From the beginning of his bachelor's degree in engineering, he has been an active developer. He had already contributed a lot to the web community when he further got involved in game development at his brother's request. He has over a year's worth of experience working with game engines such as Unity 3D, CryENGINE 3.5, and UDK. Presently, as the final phase of his Engineering degree, he is working on his industrial internship with 4play as the Chief Game Officer and is also working as a research assistant with Dr. Aynur Unal from Stanford, Palo Alto.

www.PacktPub.com

Support files, eBooks, discount offers, and more

You might want to visit www.PacktPub.com for support files and downloads related to your book.

Did you know that Packt offers eBook versions of every book published, with PDF and ePub files available? You can upgrade to the eBook version at www.PacktPub.com and as a print book customer, you are entitled to a discount on the eBook copy. Get in touch with us at service@packtpub.com for more details.

At www.PacktPub.com, you can also read a collection of free technical articles, sign up for a range of free newsletters and receive exclusive discounts and offers on Packt books and eBooks.

http://PacktLib.PacktPub.com

Do you need instant solutions to your IT questions? PacktLib is Packt's online digital book library. Here, you can access, read and search across Packt's entire library of books.

Why Subscribe?

- Fully searchable across every book published by Packt
- Copy and paste, print and bookmark content
- On demand and accessible via web browser

Free Access for Packt account holders

If you have an account with Packt at www.PacktPub.com, you can use this to access PacktLib today and view nine entirely free books. Simply use your login credentials for immediate access.

Table of Contents

Preface

Today, making games is easier than ever before. There are a plethora of game engines available for developers, and most of them can even be tried out free of charge or used to release games noncommercially. So, irrespective of whether you are modifying an already released game, building your own indie game, or maybe working on a big AAA production, the chances that you will be using a licensed 3D engine such as the popular CryENGINE are pretty big.

The times where development teams would write their custom game engine to produce a game are mostly over. The use of licensed 3D engines is very common and saves developers and publishers a lot of money. Using a licensed 3D engine instead of building a custom solution allows developers to focus on making a great game instead of developing and maintaining their own technology.

A result of this continually advancing technology development, however, is that it has become very difficult for developers to really master all aspects of a 3D engine. Engines such as CryENGINE are not simply rendering programs that are capable of drawing beautiful content on the screen in real time. Animation systems, physics simulation, AI behaviors, or particle systems are just a few parts of what makes up the CryENGINE. However, with the increasing complexity of game engines, it has become more difficult for today's game developers to stay on top of the technology.

This is where *Mastering CryENGINE* comes in. This book focuses on the professional CryENGINE developer and tries to provide an inside scoop on how to produce games at an AAA production level. Getting the most out of the engine and becoming a highly productive CryENGINE developer requires knowledge of the multitude of subsystems that CryENGINE offers.

The goal of this book is to provide you with valuable information about the most important aspects of CryENGINE production as well as guide you through the most common technical problems encountered when developing game content with the engine.

What this book covers

This book covers a wide range of topics that are closely related to making games with CryENGINE at a professional level. Basic elements such as setting up the engine, building simple environments, or other topics that might be of interest for beginners might be touched upon, but they will not be covered in too much depth. Instead, this book focuses on arming you with in-depth knowledge of the core systems of CryENGINE that are necessary to build high-quality content.

Chapter 1, Setting Up the Perfect Pipeline, focuses on one of the most important aspects of game production: a stable and flexible pipeline. This chapter covers the tailoring of the perfect pipeline for your project as well as the important aspects of setting up a new pipeline.

Chapter 2, Using the CryENGINE Input System – Keyboard, Mouse, and Game Controller, provides an overview of the CryENGINE input systems. You will learn how to create new action maps and handle user profiles as well as how to react to input events in code and flow graphs.

Chapter 3, Building Complex Flow Graph Logic, focuses on the more advanced features of the flow graph system. Nested flow graphs as well as graph tokens will be explained in detail and will be used to build a practical game example.

Chapter 4, Morphs and Bones – Creating a Facial Setup for Your Character, covers all the steps necessary to create a complete facial setup for a character. You will learn about facial libraries as well as how to get a character ready for lip syncing and procedural blinking.

Chapter 5, Mastering Sandbox, focuses on increasing your production speed, efficiency, and productivity when working with CryENGINE. Hidden features, important shortcuts, and relevant engine settings will be discussed in this chapter.

Chapter 6, Utilizing Lua Script in CryENGINE, teaches you how to use the Lua scripting language to build more sophisticated gameplay elements. The creation of new script binds and modification of the existing entities will be covered here.

Chapter 7, Animating Characters, will explain the principles of CryMannequin, the high-level animation system of CryENGINE. You will also learn how to extend the state machine to trigger your own mannequin animation sequences. The chapter will also cover other methods of triggering animations.

Chapter 8, Mastering the Smart Objects System, will provide an insight on how to use the SmartObject system. This system will be used to build a gameplay example of a security guard AI behavior. Furthermore, navigational SmartObject systems will be used to set up AI characters that can climb over walls.

Chapter 9, Eye Candy – Particles, Lens Flares, and More, focuses on adding some eye candy to your game. The setup and usage of particle effects as well as the brand new Lens Flare editor will be covered.

Chapter 10, Shipping the Build, focuses on getting your game ready to ship. It will cover how to prepare the build for release, remove unwanted source files, and reduce the overall build size.

What you need for this book

In order to make best use of the examples in this book, you should use the latest version of CryENGINE. Although much of the knowledge provided in this book can still be applied to older versions of the engine, it is recommended that you use this book with CryENGINE 3.5.2 or above.

The jump to CryENGINE 3.5

The CryENGINE technology has been around for over 10 years and the engine has undergone a lot of changes and improvements over those years.

Crytek released the latest version of the engine, CryENGINE 3, in 2009, which introduced a lot of improvements (for example, a deferred rendering pipeline) and brought the engine to XBOX 360 and PlayStation 3. Along with the addition of countless new rendering features, the Sandbox editor also underwent a big facelift.

Within the lifespan of CryENGINE 3, there has been one big transition: the jump from Version 3.4.5 to Version 3.5.

With the upgrade to Version 3.5, all the changes and improvements made during the development of the critically acclaimed games, *Crysis 3* and *Ryse*, found their way into the CryENGINE 3 SDK.

All the new features that made *Crysis 3* and *Ryse* look so stunning became available to developers with this upgrade. An improved rendering pipeline and the new animation system CryMannequin, which replaced AnimationGraph, are two of the biggest changes done to the engine in Version 3.5.

Most of the topics covered in this book will still be valuable for you if you are working with an older version of the engine. However, some of the newer features discussed in this book, for example the LensFlare editor, might not be available for you if you are working with an older version of the engine.

Other required software

In order to follow the examples in this book, we recommend that you obtain the following software:

- CryENGINE SDK 3.5.2 or above
- Photoshop Version 4 or above
- Notepad++
- Visual Studio 2010
- 3D Studio Max 2010

Who this book is for

This book is aimed at an experienced CryENGINE developer. Although it is certainly possible to use this book as a beginner who is unfamiliar with the CryENGINE technology, it will be much more efficient when a certain level of experience with the engine is there.

Whether you are a CryENGINE enthusiast looking to turn your hobby into a full-time profession or you've just started working with CryENGINE on a professional project, this book will provide you with valuable information and deep insights into the engine. This is invaluable to produce content at a professional level.

Conventions

In this book, you will find a number of styles of text that distinguish between different kinds of information. Here are some examples of these styles, and an explanation of their meaning.

Code words in text, database table names, folder names, filenames, file extensions, pathnames, dummy URLs, user input, and Twitter handles are shown as follows: "The OnReset() function will be called every time the entity script is reloaded."

A block of code is set as follows:

```
if (slot == 0) then
   self:DrawSlot(0, 1);
   self:DrawSlot(1, 0);
else
   self:DrawSlot(0, 0);
   self:DrawSlot(1, 1);
end
```

When we wish to draw your attention to a particular part of a code block, the relevant lines or items are set in bold:

```
if (slot == 0) then
  self:DrawSlot(0, 1);
  self:DrawSlot(1, 0);
else
  self:DrawSlot(0, 0);
  self:DrawSlot(1, 1);
end
```

New terms and **important words** are shown in bold. Words that you see on the screen, in menus or dialog boxes for example, appear in the text like this: "Clicking on **Show Log File** will open the respective logfile for you automatically."

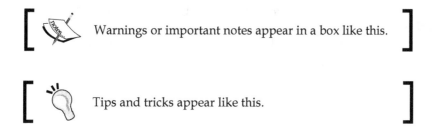

Warnings or important notes appear in a box like this.

Tips and tricks appear like this.

Reader feedback

Feedback from our readers is always welcome. Let us know what you think about this book—what you liked or may have disliked. Reader feedback is important for us to develop titles that you really get the most out of.

To send us general feedback, simply send an e-mail to feedback@packtpub.com, and mention the book title via the subject of your message.

If there is a topic that you have expertise in and you are interested in either writing or contributing to a book, see our author guide on www.packtpub.com/authors.

Customer support

Now that you are the proud owner of a Packt book, we have a number of things to help you to get the most from your purchase.

Downloading the example code

You can download the example code files for all Packt books you have purchased from your account at http://www.packtpub.com. If you purchased this book elsewhere, you can visit http://www.packtpub.com/support and register to have the files e-mailed directly to you.

Errata

Although we have taken every care to ensure the accuracy of our content, mistakes do happen. If you find a mistake in one of our books—maybe a mistake in the text or the code—we would be grateful if you would report this to us. By doing so, you can save other readers from frustration and help us improve subsequent versions of this book. If you find any errata, please report them by visiting http://www.packtpub.com/submit-errata, selecting your book, clicking on the **errata submission form** link, and entering the details of your errata. Once your errata are verified, your submission will be accepted and the errata will be uploaded on our website, or added to any list of existing errata, under the Errata section of that title. Any existing errata can be viewed by selecting your title from http://www.packtpub.com/support.

Piracy

Piracy of copyright material on the Internet is an ongoing problem across all media. At Packt, we take the protection of our copyright and licenses very seriously. If you come across any illegal copies of our works, in any form, on the Internet, please provide us with the location address or website name immediately so that we can pursue a remedy.

Please contact us at copyright@packtpub.com with a link to the suspected pirated material.

We appreciate your help in protecting our authors, and our ability to bring you valuable content.

Questions

You can contact us at questions@packtpub.com if you are having a problem with any aspect of the book, and we will do our best to address it.

1
Setting Up the Perfect Pipeline

Before the actual work on any new project can begin, you as a developer have to think about your production pipeline. Time spent on designing a robust pipeline is always time well invested. The larger the project ahead of you, the more important it is to set up a stable pipeline. In this chapter, we will discuss the following topics:

- Production pipeline setup for CryENGINE projects
- Using version control in CryENGINE projects
- Setting up automated builds and build scripts
- Integration of CryENGINE builds and versions

The goal of this chapter is to provide you with information and best practices on building a stable and flexible CryENGINE production pipeline.

What is a production pipeline?

In simple words, a CryENGINE production pipeline could be described as a series of operations you are performing with the engine in order to create your product. Things like exporting a 3D asset of compiling C++ code, for example, are parts of a typical CryENGINE pipeline. Our production pipeline also defines how and to what standards you perform all project-related tasks.

When working with CryENGINE, those project-related tasks can include:

- Exporting a 3D asset
- Compiling code
- Creating automatic builds

- Processing bug reports
- Checking files into your version control system

A pipeline is basically a number of rules and guidelines you set for yourself and your team to work on your project. If those rules make sense and fit your project, your life will become a lot easier. If they do not fit your project or if they do not exist yet, you will have a higher chance of running into all kinds of problems.

Importance of a strong pipeline

No matter what CryENGINE project you are about to start, you will have weeks or possibly months of work ahead of you. Being as prepared as you can for this should be your goal. Planning and preparing your pipeline will help you save time and work more efficiently during the lifespan of your whole project.

A well thought out pipeline, which is standardized and enforced within your team, will increase production speed significantly. In this chapter, we will discuss the most important aspects of a CryENGINE production pipeline.

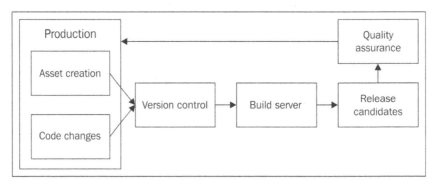

Overview of the production pipeline

Version control for CryENGINE projects

The decision of which **version control system (VCS)** to use is one of the most important pipeline decisions to make when you are planning your CryENGINE project.

It is also one of the first things that should be discussed, since a lot of other aspects of your production will depend on it.

What version control does for you

Version control is incredibly useful in any area of game production. What a VCS basically does is keep track of changes made to your files and allows you to review those changes and even helps you revert to the older versions of your files.

This means if you make a mistake or delete or lose a file, it is generally very easy to recover whatever you have lost. In addition to this, using a VCS makes it a lot easier to collaborate since you will always have an overview of what changes your team members made to the project files.

Production without version control

Even today, where VCSs such as SVN, Perforce, or Git have become very affordable, or even free, there are still teams out there working without the safety net of a version control system.

[Not using any version control whatsoever is always a bad decision for larger projects.]

Working from a shared folder

One method often used by less experienced mod teams is to work out of a shared folder, which is accessible for everybody from the network. While it might seem simple and easy to work this way with everybody just copying their files into the shared folder, there are a lot of things which can go wrong, which are as follows:

- Files can get overwritten accidently
- Code and script conflicts cannot be caught and resolved easily
- Tracing back older changes becomes extremely difficult

With low cost version control systems being widely available today, there is no reason even for small teams to work this way. Setting up and maintaining a version control solution will of course consume a certain amount of time, but it is always time well invested.

Let's have a look at a real-life example. You are working on a CryENGINE game project and you discover a game breaking bug. Let's say someone on your team submitted something which broke the game. Now it is up to you to identify and fix the issue. Having no access to either the file history or changes done to the individual files will make it very difficult for you to solve the issue. However, in a project environment with a VCS setup, you could simply step backwards through the submitted changes to identify the file which was responsible for breaking your game.

Selecting a VCS for CryENGINE projects

When it comes to deciding which VCS to use for your CryENGINE project, your decision will be determined by your budget, the scale of your project, and possibly your personal preference.

You will have to choose between a centralized and distributed VCS. While a centralized VCS keeps all files on a central server, a distributed VCS mirrors the whole repository on each client. Both systems come with different upsides and downsides, but for CryENGINE, it makes no difference which type of system is used.

There are many VCSs available today, and they come in many flavors. Most commonly used VCSs for CryENGINE projects are as follows:

- **Perforce**: This is sometimes also called P4 and is a professional centralized VCS, which mostly is the tool of choice for professional and larger size game teams. Perforce licenses are generally not free, but there are various license options which allow indie and mod teams to make use of the software without spending much money. CryENGINE has native support for Perforce and allows you to check in/out files directly from Sandbox.

- **SVN**: This is also called Subversion and is a free, open source centralized VCS. It is widely used by smaller teams without a big budget, since it can be used without any cost.

- **Git**: This is also a free to use open source VCS. It differs from Perforce and SVN by using a distributed architecture. In direct comparison to Perforce and SVN, Git can be quite difficult to use, especially for developers with a nontechnical background.

Setting up version control for CryENGINE

Once you have made your decision regarding which version control system to use for your project, it is time to set up your CryENGINE environment. Depending on your role in your game's production, certain aspects of this setup might be more or less interesting to you. For example, if you are a programmer, you might be less interested to learn about setting up your Photoshop or 3ds Max and skip ahead to the relevant coding topics.

Sandbox

Being able to check out levels, layers, or materials files directly from Sandbox without switching to your version control client is very comfortable and will speed up your workflow considerably.

Support for Perforce version control is integrated into the Sandbox editor. Sandbox will automatically check out the corresponding files when they are being modified.

When using SVN, Git, or any other system, files cannot be directly checked in/out from Sandbox. In this case, no further setup is necessary.

Perforce setup

The first step to setting up Sandbox to work with Perforce is to enable version control. This is done in the Sandbox preferences as follows:

1. Open the **Preferences** window from the **Tools** menu.

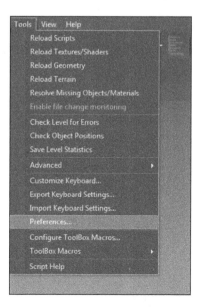

2. In the **Preferences** menu, go to **General Settings | General**.

3. Make sure the **Enable Source Control** checkbox is checked.

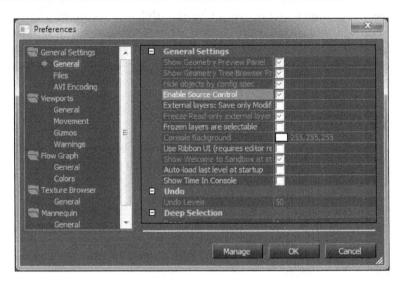

This will tell Sandbox to use version control for file operations. CryENGINE will get the Perforce server information from the Windows' environment settings and you don't need to set them up manually. To review these environment settings in Perforce, click on **Environment Settings** in the **Connection** menu as seen in the following screenshot:

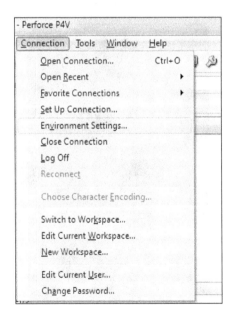

You can change the **Server** and **Workspace** settings here as seen in the following screenshot:

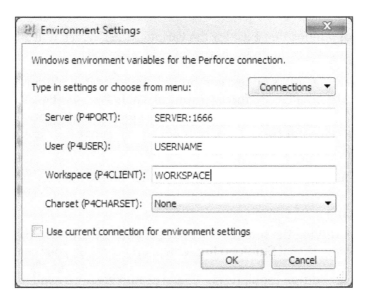

Once all your version control options are set up for CryENGINE, you will see a window as seen in the following screenshot when saving your level:

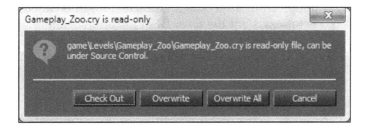

This is CryENGINE telling you that the level you are trying to save is write protected and probably version controlled. At this point, you have the choice to either overwrite your level files or check them out from Perforce.

Exploring digital content creation tools such as Photoshop and 3ds Max

When creating content for CryENGINE projects, you will most likely be using tools such as Photoshop, 3ds Max, or Maya to create 3D assets, animations, and textures.

While those tools are not directly connected to CryENGINE, it still makes sense to set them up to connect to the same version control system that is storing your code and level files.

There are a lot of plugins that exist for the various VCSs, which will allow you to check out files directly from Photoshop, Max, Maya, or XSI.

Perforce, for example, offers quite a comprehensive free set of plugins for all major tools on their website called **Perforce Graphical Tools Plug-in (P4GT)**. This is basically a big collection of plugins for all kinds of tools and systems. You can find it at `http://www.perforce.com/product/components/perforce-plugin-graphical-tools`.

For SVN and Git, there are several plugins available on the internet as well.

Visual Studio

If you will be modifying the source code of CryENGINE for your project, you will most likely be using Visual Studio to implement and compile your changes.

There is a Perforce add-on for all recent Visual Studio versions available. This plugin will automatically check out source files when modified, and add newly created files to the repository. This can save a lot of time when working with the source code.

The plugin can be installed from within the GUI of Visual Studio. To do so, open the **Extension Manager** option from the **Tools** menu. The plugin is called **P4VS**. The fastest way to find it is to search for the term *P4* in the online gallery.

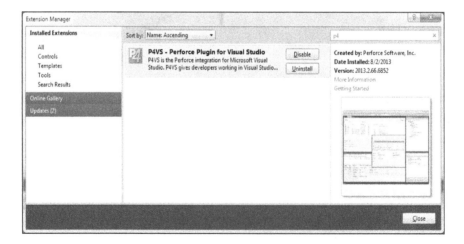

After installation, you have to activate the plugin in the Visual Studio options. In the menu **Tools**, choose **Options**. Then navigate to the section called **Source Control**. In the subsection **Plug-in Selection**, open the drop-down box and select **P4VS**. Then you can configure your connection settings.

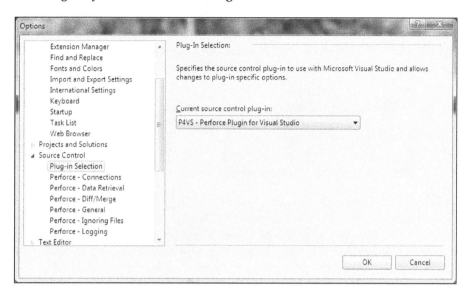

 All pictures are taken from the Visual Studio Version 2010 and might differ slightly from other versions.

Notepad

When editing text files, such as XML or Lua files, you will likely use a text editor. We recommend **Notepad++** or **Microsoft XML Notepad 2007** as it has syntax highlighting and a range of helpful plugins, such as an XML syntax checker. There is also a plugin available for Perforce. When installed, this plugin will automatically check out files when you edit them and add them to the default change list in Perforce.

The plugin can be installed through the Plugin Manager in Notepad++. It can be opened via the **Plugins** menu. Choose the plugin called **Perforce actions** from the list of available plugins and select **Install**.

Just like CryENGINE, the plugin will work with the Perforce environment settings, which can be set up via the GUI as described in the section *Setting up version control for CryENGINE*.

Identifying CryENGINE project files to be excluded from version control

Only because you are making use of a VCS, you do not need to add every single file of your CryENGINE project to the depot. Checking in files that should not be version controlled can actually be counterproductive to your workflow. It is important to know which type of files to keep out of your VCS. Generally, all files created during the build process should never be checked in.

 To keep your build clean, you should avoid checking files into your VCS that are automatically generated during the build process.

The files which are usually never checked into a VCS are as follows:

- **.DDS files**: These are generated automatically by the CryENGINE resource compiler. You should not create a .DDS file manually and check them into your VCS. The engine will take any existing .TIF file found in your project and compile an optimized .DDS texture, which will be used during runtime. When those .DDS files are locked and write protected by a VCS, they cannot be overwritten by the resource compiler. When this happens, your build will start using .DDS files, which can cause rendering problems and graphical artifacts.

- **Binaries**: Usually, CryENGINE executable files such as the GameSDK.exe, Editor.exe, and the various CryENGINE .DLL files are not checked into your VCS since they are regularly built by your project's coders, locally on their machines. While all source code files should always be checked in, those executables will normally be rebuilt every day and do not need to be checked in.

- **.GFX files**: When **Scaleform** is being used in production, .GFX files will be created by **gfx-exporter**. Those files should not be checked in but ought to be generated automatically during the build process. The gfx exporter might generate .DDS files as part of the .GFX export process for certain files, hence this step should be done as part of the automated build process.

Automated builds and build scripts

Having a system in place to create CryENGINE project builds automatically on a regular schedule can be very useful. Having the ability to switch back and forth between older and newer builds can be vital when hunting down difficult-to-fix bugs and other problems.

Although CryENGINE builds can be created manually and then copied to a storage location, it is much easier to set up a system to automate these tasks.

Creating nightly builds

Professional game development teams often have a procedure in place to create so called *nightly builds*. Those are builds created by a build server every night and distributed to the team the next morning. Level designers, artists, and other developers who do not directly work with C++ code or scripts are very comfortable working with nightly builds.

Those team members can just copy a fresh build every morning and can rely on the fact that everything has been properly compiled with all the latest code changes, and all .DDS files are properly created by the resource compiler. These automated builds can also serve as release candidates for your project and be used for QA testing.

Setting up a build server

In order to create automatic builds, you need to set up and configure a build server first. Your build server can be anything from a regular PC to a specifically designated workstation. Unless you are working on a really large scale project, any regular PC will do the job. You do not need to buy expensive server hardware if you are just intending to make a couple of builds per day.

In larger production environments where one build server has to handle builds for multiple large projects, stronger hardware will be needed, while for a single project with only one or two automatically generated builds per day, a normal desktop PC will do the job. Build servers for larger team sizes usually compile the code several times a day in order to catch bad check-ins as fast as possible. The more the coders work on the codebase, the more frequently should the server run the auto compilation. Professional teams of larger size will usually have dedicated personnel responsible for setting up the build servers and creating and maintaining build scripts called build engineers.

Your build server should not be the same PC you are working on, since the process of compiling a build will of course slow your machine down considerably. Using a dedicated build server rather than a local workstation also eliminates the risk of local changes ending up in an automated build.

Operating systems

Since the build process requires you to run the CryENGINE resource compiler as part of the asset compilation process, the build server should be running a version of Microsoft Windows. The CryENGINE resource compiler currently runs only on Microsoft Windows operating systems. Using Microsoft Windows also has the advantage that you can use the Windows scheduler to have your build scripts run automatically every night.

What build scripts should do

Once you have your build server hardware set up, it is time to create a set of build scripts, which will take care of automatically producing builds for you. Your goal will be to create a build script which takes all the latest changes done to your project by all team members and compile a new and clean build from them. Your build script should perform the following tasks:

- Gathering all the latest C++ code and Lua scripts
- Generating .DDS files for all existing .TIF files
- Distributing the completed build to a central network location

Depending on your project, there could be several optional tasks you might want your build scripts to perform, such as the following:

- Performing automated performance tests
- Creating automated level benchmarks
- Exporting all your game's levels
- Uploading an archived version of the build to an FTP location
- Creating change logs containing all changes done

A typical build process looks like this:

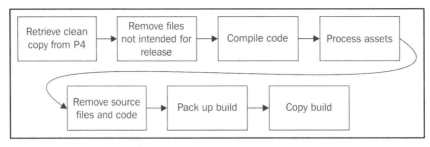

Overview of the build process

Creating your custom build script

Now it is time to get your hands dirty and create your own build script. But don't worry, you won't have to write it all on your own, since you will be provided with a sample build script, which you can use as a base and modify to suit your needs. There is a variety of scripting languages available you could use to create your build scripts. In the following example, we are using simple batch files. Of course, you are free to use a more sophisticated scripting language, such as Python.

For this example build script, we are using Perforce and some additional software, specifically:

- Beyond Compare 3
- WinRAR
- Visual Studio 2010
- Python 3.0 or higher

 There is no need to go out and buy all this software if you just want to test the build scripts. You can just use the trial versions of the software and then decide later whether you would like to keep on using them.

Before starting with the actual scripts, the computer that will function as the build server needs to be set up properly. The following steps need to be done:

1. Install the following software:
    - Beyond Compare 3
    - WinRAR
    - Perforce
    - Visual Studio 2010
    - Python 3.0 or higher

2. Set up a Perforce user for use in the build script, called a **buildbot**.
3. Create a folder for the build scripts.
4. Create a folder for the builds to be stored.
5. Download and extract the build script bundle from *<webadress>*.
6. Modify the settings inside `CreateFullBuild.bat` with your data.

The example build scripts provided in this book require the use of a so-called Diff software. In the examples provided here, we use the software Beyond Compare 3. The software can be downloaded from `http://www.scootersoftware.com/download.php`.

Of course, different types of software can be used and you will just need to adjust the appropriate portions of the build script. In order to follow the examples provided in this book, the free trial version of Beyond Compare 3 will be sufficient.

This section assumes that you have a physical build server and a VCS set up already. We will be using Perforce in our example build scripts, but you can easily adjust the scripts to use SVN, Git, or any other VCS instead.

Let's have a look at the tasks that the build bot needs to perform:

- Getting the latest code and assets from Perforce
- Coping relevant data to a work folder
- Compiling the code in 32- and 64-bit
- Compiling the assets
- Creating the PAK files
- Packing up the code
- Moving build to the target folder

The actual build script is rather long, so let's break it down into smaller sections and look at each section individually. To make it easier for you, the places in the script that you need to change and replace with your own folder names and project dependent settings will be pointed out in detail.

In your production environment, you can use the files from this script bundle or write your own.

Writing your own script

To write your own script, start by creating a new text file inside your build scripts folder and call it `CreateBuild.bat`. Then edit it with a text editing program, such as Notepad++ and copy or type the script lines from this book. To make things easier, a text editor with syntax highlighting should be used.

The purpose of this first part of the script is just to print out some status information as follows:

```
@echo off
cls
```

```
echo.
echo Creating a new full projectbuild
echo---------------------------------
echoNew build started at: %date% %time%
```

Downloading the example code

You can download the example code files for all Packt books you have purchased from your account at http://www.packtpub.com. If you purchased this book elsewhere, you can visit http://www.packtpub.com/support and register to have the files e-mailed directly to you.

These first six lines are simply clearing the console and printing the current time and date onto the screen (or into a logfile). Nothing is actually happening yet. You can safely delete and modify these lines as you like.

Printing out console output is always helpful as it gives some feedback as to where in the script the process currently is. A full build on a regular PC can take over an hour, depending on the amount of assets that need to be compiled. Knowing the current stage of the build process can be helpful to you.

These outputs will give you an insight on where your build failed if it was unsuccessful.

The next lines of the script focus on a general folder setup as follows:

```
G:
setBuildBotPath=G:\p4\Build_Server\BuildScripts
setBuildWorkPath=G:\BuildArchive\Build_InProgress
setBuildSourcePath=G:\p4\Build_Server\ProjectName
set BuildTargetPath=G:\BuildArchive\ProjectName_%date:~10,4%_%date:~4,
2%_%date:~7,2%
setVisualStudioPath=C:\Program Files\Microsoft Visual Studio 2010\
Common7\IDE
setBeyondComparePath= C:\Program Files\Beyond Compare 3\BComp.com
setWinRarPath=C:\Program Files\WinRAR\Winrar.exe
```

The first command in this block of code sets the drive that the build scripts and work in progress folder for the build will be located in; in our case, this is the G drive. You will need to adjust this to the drive that your temporary build folder is located in (as set in `BuildWorkPath`).

The next four lines set the folder paths that are relevant for the build server. You will need to adjust each of these to point to your own folders.

`BuildBotPath` should point to the folder that contains the build scripts, the preceding script included. The script will need to call helper scripts and expects these to be located in this folder. Specifying a script path at the beginning of the script makes it easy to create custom versions of the build scripts for different projects on the same server.

`BuildSourcePath` is the path to where the local repository of the project is located on the hard disk of the build server. In case the build server is also used as a work machine, this should not be the path to the local work directory. The build bot should have its own login and local work directory for the versioning system.

`BuildWorkPath` is a temporary folder that is only used for copying and compiling the build. After it is done, it will be moved to a final target folder. This folder is usually shared on a network drive. The move to the final folder doesn't happen until the entire build script is done, to avoid users copying down unfinished builds.

`BuildTargetPath` is the final target folder for the build. This will be autogenerated from the project name and the current date. If you are planning on having more than one build per day, you could consider adding a time stamp to the folder. This autogenerated folder name will make sorting the builds by date very simple.

Lastly, you will need to provide the installation locations for Beyond Compare 3, WinRar, and Visual Studio, in the variables `VisualStudioPath`, `VisualStudioPath`, and `WinRarPath` respectively.

Getting the latest files from your version control

Now, it's time to update the code and assets from Perforce as follows:

```
echo.
echo Retrieving the latest from the version control
p4 -c WORKSPACE -p PERFORCE_SERVER:1666 -P PASSWORD -u USERNAME login
p4 sync -q //PROJECTNAME/...#head
echo Done.
```

In this part of the script, you will need to replace everything that is printed in *CAPITAL* letters with your own version control data. The `//PROJECTNAME/` term in the fourth line is the depot path of your repository that you want to retrieve. If you have chosen SVN or Git as your version control software, you will need to replace the appropriate calls.

If you are using your PC as a work station and build server simultaneously, and have more than one workspace mapped to the same machine, you might need to change the lines to the following, since the environment variables will probably not be set to the build server's user and workspace. This also applies if you don't have a password set up for your build bot user, as follows:

```
p4 -c WORKSPACE -u USERNAME sync -q //PROJECTNAME/...#head
```

Now it is time to copy all the relevant data into the temporary work folder and compile it. This folder might or might not exist yet. If it does, it needs to be cleared first so that no old data mixes with the new clean build as follows:

```
if exist "%BuildWorkPath%" (
echo.
echoClearing out temporary Work Folder
echo %BuildWorkPath%
rmdir /S /Q "%BuildWorkPath%"
)
```

Next, the data can be copied from the local repository folder to the work folder as follows:

```
echo.
echo Copy build relevant data
echo to %BuildWorkPath%
mkdir "%BuildWorkPath%"
cd %BuildBotPath%
%BeyondComparePath%/closescript "@CopyBuildScript.txt"
echoDone.
```

This bit of the script calls upon **Beyond Compare**, a folder diff tool, to copy the build into the work folder. This is done because not all of the files from the repository are required for the build. Source assets, for example, Photoshop, 3ds Max, or ZBrush files need to be removed. These files are commonly rather large and would unnecessarily bloat up the build size. Also, the build server's task is to create release candidates, and source assets are usually not shipped.

Beyond Compare 3 can filter out all files that are not desired in the final released build. The script bundle available for download with this book includes a script that filters out the most common source asset types. The script is called `CopyBuildScript.txt` and is called upon in the preceding script block.

If Beyond Compare 3 is installed in a different location on your computer, you will need to adjust the path to `BComp.com` in the script. If you are using a different folder diff tool, you can replace this part completely with the appropriate calls to your tool.

Another function the script performs is to remove the read-only flag on all copied files. Many version control systems such as Perforce set a read-only flag on all files in the local repository unless they are checked out, and the script takes care of this. The files need to be writable so that build script can compile, pack, and delete files later.

Compiling the code

Now the code can finally be compiled as follows:

```
echo.
mkdir "%BuildWorkPath%\Logfiles"
cd %BuildWorkPath%\Code\Solutions

echo Compiling 64 Bit
"%VisualStudioPath%\devenv.com" CryEngine.sln /rebuild "Profile|x64" >
"%BuildWorkPath%\Logfiles\Log_64Bit.txt"
echo Compiling 32 Bit
"%VisualStudioPath%\devenv.com" CryEngine.sln /rebuild "Profile|Win32"
> "%BuildWorkPath%\Logfiles\Log_32Bit.txt"
echo Done.
```

The first half of this script block creates a subfolder within the build folder to store the logfiles in. This is optional but can be very useful if there are any compilation errors for either code or assets. It is a good first place to start looking in when a build fails.

Next, the command-line version of the Visual Studio compiler is called upon to compile the first 64-bit and then 32-bit of the project.

Then, the path to the Visual Studio installation is set to the default installation location. If your Visual Studio is installed in a different directory, you will need to adjust this path.

You will also need to replace the CryEngine.sln filename with your own solution filename should you change it.

Logfiles will be saved to the Logfiles subfolder. The FreeSDK release solution file is usually named differently than the full source release.

At the time of writing this book, the default solution file for the CryENGINE release requires the Visual Studio 2010 compilers. Future releases of CryENGINE might require Visual Studio 2012 or up. You will need to adjust the folder path in this case.

Compiling the code will create temporary files, such as for example *.pdb* files containing debug information. These files need to be removed as they should not be part of a release candidate. They would increase the build size and could potentially be used to reverse engineer your code.

The following part of our build script will remove these files and folders:

```
echo.
echo Removing temporary files from Code Build
cd %BuildWorkPath%\Bin32
del *.lib
del *.pdb
del *.exp
delCryAction.map
cd %BuildWorkPath%\Bin64
del *.lib
del *.pdb
del *.exp
delCryAction.map
cd %BuildWorkPath%
rmdir /S /Q BinTemp
```

These instructions are for a full source build of CryENGINE. If only the game code is compiled, the lines concerning Cry Action can be removed.

 Instead of deleting the map and pdb files, you can also choose to archive them somewhere on your server. This will allow you to track down crashes that are reported from your end users, if they submit you a callstack.

Compiling the assets

The code is compiled now, so it is time to take care of the assets as follows:

```
echo.
echo Compile Assets
cd %BuildWorkPath%
echo Compiling Objects...
.\Bin32\RC\rc.exe .\Game\Objects\* /p=PC /ext_dds /ext_cba /recursive
/threads=cores /processes=cores > ".\Logfiles\AssetCompilationLog_
Objects.txt"
echo Compiling Libs...
.\Bin32\RC\rc.exe .\Game\Libs\* /p=PC /ext_dds /ext_cba/recursive /
threads=cores /processes=cores > ".\Logfiles\AssetCompilationLog_Libs.
txt"
```

```
echo Compiling Textures...
.\Bin32\RC\rc.exe .\Game\Textures\* /p=PC /ext_dds /ext_cba /recursive
/threads=cores /processes=cores > ".\Logfiles\AssetCompilationLog_
Textures.txt"
echo Compiling Materials...
.\Bin32\RC\rc.exe .\Game\Materials\* /p=PC /ext_dds /ext_
cba /recursive /threads=cores /processes=cores > ".\Logfiles\
AssetCompilationLog_Materials.txt"
echo Compiling Levels...
.\Bin32\RC\rc.exe .\Game\Levels\* /p=PC /ext_dds /ext_cba /recursive
/threads=cores /processes=cores > ".\Logfiles\AssetCompilationLog_
Levels.txt"
Echo Done.
```

The preceding line makes several calls to the resource compiler located by default in the RC folder under Bin32, shipped with any version of CryENGINE, to compile the assets. The resource compiler's output will be piped into a separate text file inside the Logfiles folder. Asset compilation will run over all data files (geometry, images, and so on) and process it. For images, this means compiling and converting them into platform specific and optimized .DDS files.

The XML file that contains the job description is provided with the CryENGINE build. However, if you have changed your default game folder from GameSDK to a folder of a different name, you will need to open the RCJob_Build_SDK_no_ scripts.xml file in a text editor and adjust the folder name in the default properties at the top of the file.

This step in the build process usually takes the longest. Using a build server with multiple CPU cores can significantly speed up the process. While giving a definitive speed advantage, multiple threads will create a less detailed log output. To get a log entry for every asset that was processed and error codes, remove the parameters / threads=cores /processes=cores from the call in the preceding script.

To get a list of all the console parameters for the resource compiler in a text file, type ./Bin32/RC/rc.exe /help > RCCommands.txt in the console in the build's root folder. It will create a file RCCommands. txt in the root, containing documentation for each parameter.

For projects that create automated builds several times a day, it is sensible to create a separate build script that will only compile the code and copy the already compiled assets from the last build into it, for a faster turnaround time.

After all assets are processed by the resource compiler, the now duplicate .TIF file can be removed as follows:

```
echo.
echo Remove redundant tif files
cd %BuildWorkPath%\Game
copy "%BuildBotPath%\delete_redundant_tifs.py" .\.
delete_redundant_tifs.py
del delete_redundant_tifs.py
```

After the processing of the assets, the resource compiler will have created a DDS file for all .TIF files it could find in the directories. The .TIF files are considered source files and should not be shipped to end users. They are also usually rather large and would unnecessarily bloat up the build. The Python script delete_redundant_tifs.py traverses through the game folder and its subfolders and removes all those .TIF files that have a corresponding .DDS file. This script is included in the script bundle available for download and requires Python to run.

After this clean-up step, the assets need to be compressed into PAK files:

```
echo.
echo creating PAK files and deleting original folders
cd %BuildWorkPath%\Game

echo.
echo Creating Objects.pak
"%WinRarPath%" a -r Objects.zip .\Objects
rename Objects.zip Objects.pak
rmdir /S /Q Objects

echo Creating Animations.pak
"%WinRarPath%" a -r Animations.zip .\Animations
rename Animations.zip Animations.pak
rmdir /S /Q Animations

echo Creating GameData.pak
"%WinRarPath%" a -r GameData.zip .\Entities .\Libs .\Scripts .\Prefabs
.\Fonts
rename GameData.zip GameData.pak
rmdir /S /Q Entities
rmdir /S /Q Libs
rmdir /S /Q Scripts
rmdir /S /Q Prefabs
rmdir /S /Q Fonts
```

```
echo Creating Sounds.pak
"%WinRarPath%" a -r Sounds.zip .\Music .\Sounds .\Languages .\
Localized
rename Sounds.zip Sounds.pak
rmdir /S /Q Music
rmdir /S /Q Sounds
rmdir /S /Q Languages
rmdir /S /Q Localized

echo Creating Textures.pak
"%WinRarPath%" a -r Textures.zip .\Materials .\Textures
rename Textures.zip Textures.pak
rmdir /S /Q Materials
rmdir /S /Q Textures
```

PAK files are simple ZIP files with a different ending. Common compression software, such as WinRAR and 7-Zip can open and create these files. In this example, we will use WinRAR to create the PAK files.

After each PAK file is created, the source folders are deleted with the `rmdir` commands. This setup will create five different PAK files, combining the various folders into easily shippable containers.

> It is possible to let the resource compiler compile the assets and create the PAK files automatically by using a job XML configuration file. Most CryENGINE releases ship with one or more example job XML files inside the RC folder under Bin32.
>
> These example files usually need to be heavily modified before it will work for custom builds. The names and contents of these files change with each release so they are not used in this build script example to prevent version conflicts.

After this has finished, the source code can be either packed or removed as follows:

```
echo.
echo -- Zip the Code folder (and delete) --
cd %BuildWorkPath%
"%WinRarPath%" a -r Code.zip .\Code
rmdir /S /Q Code
```

The zipped code should of course not be shipped to end users. However, it can be useful to keep the code that was used for compilation as part of the build inside the internal build archive. It sometimes becomes necessary during production to use an older build, for example, for demonstrations or for bug hunting. In these cases, it can be extremely useful to be able to access the code used for the creation of the build quickly and without version control hassle.

After this last step, the build is finished. It can now be moved to the target location, usually on a shared network drive, as follows:

```
echo.
echo -- Rename Build folder --
cd %BuildWorkPath%
cd..
move "%BuildWorkPath%" "%BuildTargetPath%"

echo.
echo Build Finished: %date% %time%
echo ====================
echo Build Done.
echo.
```

The build script developed in this chapter is by no means the single and only way to create CryENGINE builds. This should serve as base line to get you started. During the development of your project, you will most likely want to extend and customize the build scripts to better suit your needs.

Wrapping it up

The preceding build script will output some status messages onto the console it was started from. For builds started manually, this works fine. If the console output is collected as well, a simple wrapper script can call the build script and pipe its entire output into a logfile.

The following code snippet is an example of such a wrapper script. It is included in the scripts bundle and the file is called `BuildWithLogFile.bat`:

This script will create a logfile called `BuildLog.txt` and move it into the `Logfiles` folder of the newly created build after it is finished. The usage of such a wrapper script is recommended for automated builds.

```
@echo off

cls
echo Starting new Build
```

```
echo =======================================
echoLogfile will be saved to BuildLog.txt
echo Build Started: %date% %time%


callCreateBuild.bat > "BuildLog.txt"


move "%BuildBotPath%\BuildLog.txt" "%BuildTargetPath%\Logfiles\
BuildLog.txt"
echo =======================================
echo Build done.
```

Scheduling automated builds

To create builds at a fixed time during the day, we need to start the build script automatically at specified times. This can be done with the Windows Task Scheduler. This feature allows you to run certain programs or scripts repeatedly at predefined dates and times.

The task scheduler can be accessed via the Windows Control Panel. Go to **System and Security** and then find the task scheduler under the section called **Administrative Tools**.

Create a new task by selecting **Create Basic Task** from the **Actions** bar on the right. Enter a name and a brief description for the new task, for example, Daily Overnight Build.

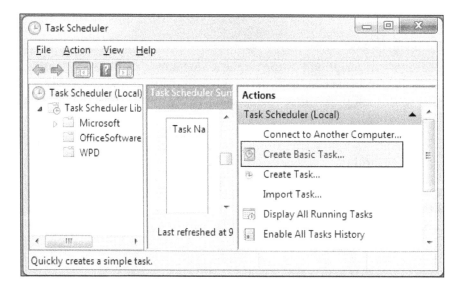

Next, you will need to specify a frequency at which to run the build script. For fulltime development projects with a dedicated build server, we recommend creating a build at least daily. For hobby projects, or projects with a smaller team size, creating weekly builds might be enough. Creating too frequent builds with very little changes in between them will only be a waste of hard disk space, so choose according to your project needs.

> Choosing the weekly frequency will give you the most customization options. After selecting this setting, you can choose the individual days of the week on which the task should run. For hobby and mod teams working mainly on the weekend, daily builds on Friday through Monday might not make so much sense. Development teams working fulltime will probably want to choose a setting of one build daily during the work week, but none on the weekends.

The task creation wizard seen in the following screenshot makes it easy to schedule automatic builds:

In many development studios, the build server will also host the version control system, internal documentation, and bug tracking services and potentially serve as a network drive.

To prevent the automated builds from causing a performance hit on the server during work hours, it is sensible to schedule the task at a time when it is most likely that no one needs the server for other purposes, such as during the night or the early morning hours.

After the frequency has been set, we can define what action should be performed when the task is executed. Choose **Start a Program** from the list and click on **Next**.

The next page of the wizard will ask you to provide the program or script that should be run. Use the **Browse** button to select the BuildWithLogFile.bat script. Also, set the path that contains the build scripts in the edit field labeled **Start in**.

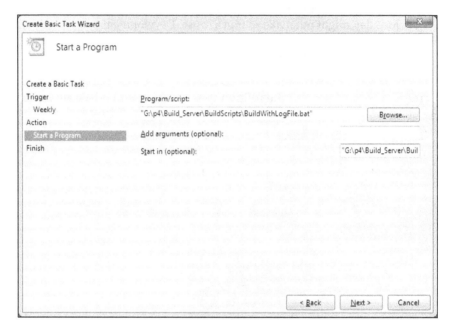

Hit **Next** and **Finish** to finalize the process. If you want to test your task, you can either set the frequency to a one-time run a few minutes from the current time, or manually select the task from the **Task Scheduler Library** and then **Run** from the right-click menu.

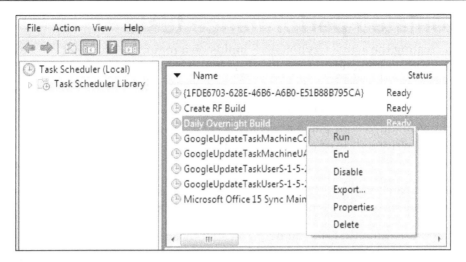

A console window should open showing the log output from the build script.

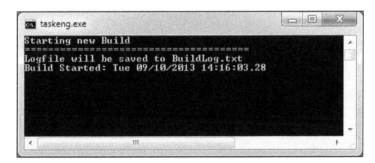

The automated task will create clean builds of your project at the set frequency for as long as you keep the task active in the task scheduler. The builds will be collected in the build archive folder you specified in the script. From time to time, you might want to go through that folder and delete older builds or archive them to another storage location.

 Don't delete all of your old builds as they can be extremely handy at the end of your development when tracking down resilient and hard-to-find bugs. Keep at least one build from every month's development to help you narrow down timeframes when a certain bug first appears. This makes the process of finding the culprit changelist a lot faster.

Automated performance tests

Besides creating the actual CryENGINE builds on a regular schedule, it can be quite useful to create automatic performance benchmarks.

CryENGINE is a high performance 3D engine, which is able to render beautiful scenes at a high frame rate. However, there is always a chance that certain changes or additions made to your game project will affect the performance negatively. A line of badly written code or a few un-optimized assets might lower your frame rate considerably.

Being able to catch those performance issues early on is very important. The sooner a performance issue can be identified, the sooner it can be fixed.

Automated performance tests can help you spot those issues as soon as they appear.

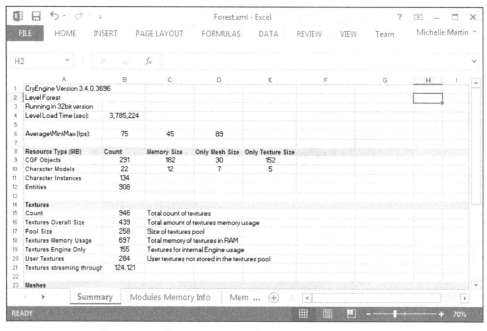

Performance file generated using the save level stats command

Using level statistics to profile the performance of a level

CryENGINE has the ability to generate so-called level statistics files, which contain a lot of information about the performance situation of the level. By reviewing and comparing those files, it is easy to identify any existing performance problems. The level statistics file for a level can be generated manually using the `savelevelstats` console command. Let's give it a try and generate a level statistics file for your level.

1. Open the level you want to profile in Sandbox.
2. Type `savelevelstats` into the console.

Depending on your computer and the size of your level, it might take several minutes to generate the level statistics file.

The higher the object count of your level, the longer the process will take. The `savelevelstats` command will collect detailed information about every object in your level, hence the higher the object count, the longer the process will take.

Once the statistics file has been generated, let's open it up and have a look at the details.

1. Go to the **.../TestResults** folder.
2. Open `levelname.xml`.

You can see that the statistics files have been generated as `.xml` files. You will need to use MS Excel to view the files. If you do not have access to MS Excel, you can just download the free Excel file viewer from `http://www.microsoft.com/en-us/download/details.aspx?id=10`.

Now, let's have a look at what has been generated. Take a moment and browse through the information contained in the files. You will see that there is a lot of relevant information contained in the documents. Everything from the overall loading time of your level up to the polygon count of individual assets can be found. You can use all this information to create a comprehensive picture of the performance situation of your build.

A more detailed description of the individual entries in the level statistics file can be found in the official CryENGINE documentation found at `http://freesdk.crydev.net`.

You might have noticed that the level statistics files we just generated, although being very comprehensive, only show a snapshot of the performance situation of our level. They provide us with performance data from just the point in time they have been created.

Only collecting performance data over a longer period of time will allow you to see certain trends and developments.

Once your build scripts are set up to generate the level statistics automatically, you could also combine the gathered information in one easy-to-read document.

Build integration

One of the bigger challenges when working with the CryENGINE codebase is integrating new versions of the CryENGINE SDK. Crytek's engine team is constantly changing and updating the engine. New features get added while others get optimized or updated. New versions of the SDK are released multiple times per year.

Although there is no need to upgrade and integrate those new versions into your projects codebase, you usually want to upgrade sooner or later, since the updates contain many new features and optimizations which will benefit your game.

Depending on the size and scope of your project, integrating new versions of the SDK can be anything from easy to very difficult.

In the next paragraph, we will be discussing the best possible way to integrate new versions of the CryENGINE SDK.

Integrating a new version of CryENGINE

When incorporating updates into your build, you will need to merge the changes made by **Crytek** with the changes made by your development team. This process is called integration. Doing this manually is no small task even in a small production environment, and becomes nearly impossible in larger teams due to the sheer number of changes made, especially to the source code.

A version control system can make this process a lot easier, as it comes equipped with integration and merging tools. If versioning was used from the start of a project, the software will have tracked a history of all changes and know how to merge them together. We will briefly describe how to set up your repository to make integration of a new CryENGINE release as easy as possible.

The engine depot

When starting with a new project, the first repository you should create is one for the unmodified CryENGINE version, the so-called vanilla build. Unless you are planning to use the assets shipped with the SDK, this repository should only contain the Entities, Scripts, and Libs folders from the release.

Do not check in any of your project changes into this repository. This depot will only serve to track the changes between the individual releases of CryENGINE.

 If you are not working with a full source license, you will be using most of the DLL files provided with the build release. In this case, it is recommended to check in all DLL files except the GameDLL file into the versioning system as well.

Project branch

Create a new branch from the engine depot that you created. The steps to create a new branch are different in every version control system. In Perforce, you can create new branches directly via the GUI. Right-click on the depot folder containing the engine and choose **Branch Files...**. Then specify a name for the new target branch and confirm by clicking on **Branch**. You can now start making your project-specific changes and also check in your project's assets.

 If you have already started on a project and don't have a version history, you can still follow this workflow. Check in the vanilla build and create a project branch as described. Then delete the contents of the newly created local project folder and copy your current project into the same folder. Then choose **Reconcile Offline Work** in the Perforce GUI to create the version history.

Integration

When a new version of CryENGINE is released, you will need to perform two steps. First you need to update the engine branch in your depot and then you need to integrate and merge those changes into your project's branch.

The cleanest way to update your engine branch is to delete the local folder and replace it with the new release. Then let the version control software run a check on the differences. This is done differently in all the software. In Perforce, you can right-click on the engine depot folder in the GUI and choose **Reconcile Offline Work**. This will generate a changelist with the engine update.

Once this changelist is checked in, you need to integrate it into your project's repository. With Perforce, this is done by right-clicking on the engine branch folder and choosing **Merge/Integrate**. Choose your project's depot as the target folder and select **Merge**. This will generate a new change list with the relevant changes. Right-click on the changelist and select **Resolve Files** to merge the changes between your project and the engine update.

Before you can check in this changelist, you will need to resolve any conflicts. A conflict happens when the version control software doesn't know how to merge a file that has been changed by both your project team and the CryENGINE update. This can happen if the same line of code in a source file has been changed, for example. In this case, you need to manually merge the file. If there are any conflicts in your changelist, you will get a message window after the preceding step gets resolved.

[Always compile the entire build and test it before you check in an engine update.]

Quality assurance processes

Having quality assurance (QA) procedures in place for your game project is important and will help to keep an overview of the problems and issues in your game. No matter how thorough your work is and how prepared you are, there will always be bugs. The quality assurance part of your production pipeline is not supposed to make sure there are no bugs, but rather help you decide how to manage the bugs you will encounter in the course of your project.

The QA workflow of your production pipeline should be tailored to the size of your project. A small two-man team working on a CryENGINE mod will require a different approach than a 100-man team working on an AAA title. Depending on your team and project size, your solution could be anything from simply writing bugs down on a piece of paper to entering bugs into an online bug tracking system.

QA pipeline in larger scale teams

First, let's have a look at how professional large scale teams set up their QA pipeline. In those types of production environments, found in most AAA studios today, a bug will go through many stages before it is finally fixed.

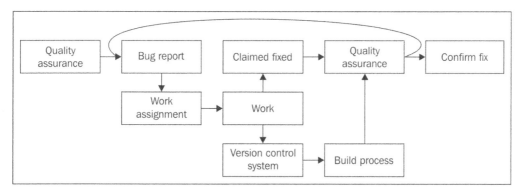

QA pipeline in larger scale teams

You can see that this process is rather complex and involves many stages and possibly various people being involved.

A bug, also commonly called an issue, gets identified, confirmed, fixed, and then finally closed. Usually a bug-tracking software such as **JIRA** or **Bugzilla** is used to manage the issues.

The benefit of this process often employed by larger-sized teams is that it is very thorough. Working this way will make sure almost every bug will get caught, documented, and fixed.

This is a good approach if you work with a development team of a larger size and need to handle larger amounts of bugs. The bug tracking system you decide to use will depend on your specific needs and your available budget.

QA pipeline in smaller teams

If you are working in a smaller team, maybe with just one or two other people, your QA approach will be a bit different. It might be sufficient for you to just write down the issue in an issue tracking system and then revisit and fix the bug at a later time.

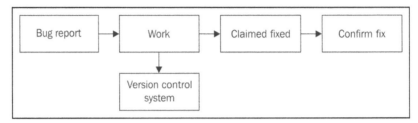

QA pipeline in smaller teams

Working without a QA pipeline

If you decide to work on your project without setting up any QA pipeline at all, you will sooner or later run into problems, since even small projects can produce a lot of bugs and issues.

Simply saying "I'll remember this bug and will fix it later" might sound easy but is not practical. No matter how thorough you are, if you do not track your issues properly, you will eventually end up shipping your game with them.

Understanding issue tracking in CryENGINE

When you create reports about new issues and bugs for your project, it is important to include as much relevant information as necessary. This will make life a lot easier for the person who has to fix the issue.

A badly written bug report can cause confusion and cost additional time. When you enter new bug reports into your bug tracking system, make sure you include all the information that is relevant in order to identify and fix the issue.

Relevant information for a CryENGINE issue includes the following:

- CryENGINE build and version number
- System specifications (hardware, DirectX version, and so on)
- The crash log and call stack if available
- The level name related to the problem (if applicable)

In addition to this, the issue should also be described as accurately as possible. The more information included, the easier it will be to fix the issue.

Summary

In this chapter, we focused on the different aspects of the CryENGINE production pipeline. You learned about the importance of planning and setting up essential elements of your pipeline including version control systems, automated builds, and quality assurance processes.

Following the guidelines and techniques detailed in this chapter will make it a lot easier for you to set up and maintain your project. You will be ready to scale your project with your team size, integrate engine updates, and stay ahead of any potential problems.

Remember that a stable and robust production pipeline is one of the most underestimated, yet most important components of your project.

Now, that all this preparation work regarding your pipeline is taken care of, things will get a bit more hands-on in the next chapter. You will get an introduction to the CryENGINE input system and learn how to modify and set up your game controls and input methods.

2
Using the CryENGINE Input System – Keyboard, Mouse, and Game Controller

For any game or simulation to be interactive, it needs to be able to react to user input to control characters, vehicles, weapons, or in-game menus. In this chapter, you will learn to use the CryENGINE input system; learn how it interfaces with input devices such as a mouse, keyboard, and game controllers; and how you can react to input events in your own game project.

The CryENGINE input system

There are several aspects of the input system in CryENGINE, but in general it can be broken down into two components. The component that takes care of the actual input devices, such as the mouse and keyboard, and the component that handles the input events coming from these devices. Before we get into the intricacies of the input system, we will take a quick look at the layer of abstraction between the actual input devices and the systems using them.

A layer of abstraction

The source code that interfaces with the individual devices is separated into its own DLL called `CryInput`. This library handles the actual communication with the input devices and their drivers. Support for a new input device would usually be implemented inside this library. Currently supported input devices are the mouse, keyboard, the Xbox 360 controller, and the PlayStation 3 controller.

The `CryInput` DLL provides a layer of abstraction between the devices themselves and the systems that react with them. The input system queries the states of all devices regularly, or listens to their events, and then sends out input events to the rest of the engine. Classes in all other DLLs can listen to these inputs and choose to react to them.

This abstraction makes handling inputs very easy on the game side. Mouse movements are different from keystrokes on the keyboard or buttons on a gamepad, and differentiating between the different types of data can be a tedious task. **CryInput** unifies this data by running it through the same input event system. This means that input from a range of completely different devices can be handled in the same way. The game code does not need to worry about how to access the various input devices and deal with drivers and interfaces, since the low level implementation of the input system takes care of that part.

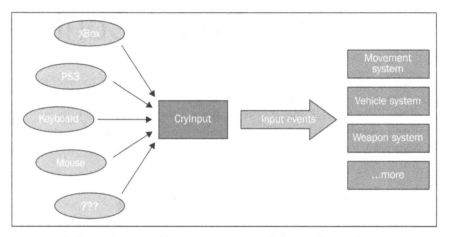

CryInput takes care of the communication with the actual input devices

The abstraction of input devices also works to our advantage when we send events to input devices, for example, to trigger force feedback on a game controller. The game logic can play rumble effects without first requesting which controllers are attached and whether they support force feedback or not. The individual device-specific code is handled by the low level input system.

The input event system

Classes and systems anywhere in CryENGINE can listen and react to events coming from the input system. There are two kinds of events that are distributed: **Input events** and **Action events**.

The Input events are generated directly from the input system. The Action events are sent from the Game Actions system inside CryAction. They represent another layer of abstraction between the input system and the game logic.

To be able to receive and react to the input of Action events, classes can register themselves as input listeners or Action listeners, or both. The differences between the direct input events and Action events will be explained in the next section.

 The common interfaces for these input events can be found in the files IInput.h and IActionMapManager.h, and they are called IInputEventListener and IActionListener.

Game actions

There are two options any game system has when it wants to react to user input. In the simplest form, the code will listen to a specific input event, such as the user pressing the Space bar on the keyboard. Whenever this event is received, the code can react with the appropriate response, for example by making the player character jump.

This direct link between a key on the keyboard and a reaction in the game world is very straightforward, but also very limited. The code will need to check whether the player character is currently allowed to jump. Triggering jumps might need to be prevented during a cut-scene, while in a vehicle, or when a menu is currently shown.

Also, nowadays it is customary to allow players to customize the keyboard layout. The key to trigger a jump might not be the Space bar after the player has personalized the controls and the code responding to the input event needs to account for that.

In addition to keyboard input, many games also offer support for game controllers. For a multiplatform project, this could even be considered a must. Game controllers might also be present on a PC, and the user might prefer using them instead of mouse and keyboard. In our example, the code that triggers the jump would also have to listen for events from those game controllers. And of course, the controller layout is usually customizable by the player as well.

All this adds up to a fair bit of managing code that would need to be written for each class that wanted to react to input events. To solve this, another layer of abstraction between the input events and the responses to them is provided by CryENGINE: the **Game Action** system that manages the so-called **Action Map** table.

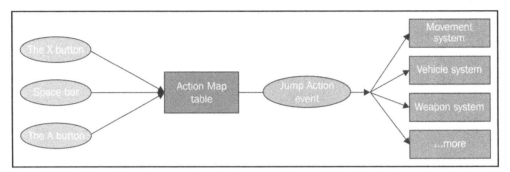

The mapping of input events to Actions provides a layer of abstraction

The Game Action system is an additional event system that links input events to Action events. The core of the system is the **ActionMapManager** that manages the Action Map tables and sits in CryAction. The system works as a simple mapping. One or more input events are mapped to an Action, for example, the Space bar on the keyboard, the *A* button on the Xbox controller, and the *X* button on the PS3 controller are all mapped to an Action event with the name jump. Whenever the Game Action system receives either of these three input events, it will send out the jump Action event. Game systems can listen to Action events and respond to them, rather than listen to the input events directly.

Action Maps

As described in the preceding player-jumping example, listening to Actions has the benefit that the code responding to the events doesn't need to be concerned with controller and input mapping. Since the mapping can be changed, this is a distinct advantage over listening for? input events directly. This is all done in the Game Actions system within the CryAction DLL.

The mapping of input events to Action events, that is, which keys and controller buttons trigger which Actions, is done inside a large table called an Action Map. Action Maps are stored in the XML file format.

One of the advantages of Action Maps is that they can be modified by the player. Actions can be rebound to different input events and the modified Action Map can be saved. Every game might not offer this functionality, of course, and you will need to decide whether this will make sense for your specific project. The *User profiles* section will explain how to modify an **ActionMap** at runtime, as well as saving and loading them.

Regardless of whether your game will allow the controls to be customized by the players, it will need to ship with a default ActionMap, a default mapping of input events to Action events. For this, you will need a list of Action events that can be triggered and a mapping that binds input events to them. You will not need to create this from scratch, however, since the CryENGINE SDK ships with both. You can extend and modify the existing files to meet the needs of your project.

The default Action Map is stored in the `defaultprofile.xml` file at `Game/Libs/config`. This file contains the default mapping for all the Action events you need, and it will not change after shipping. This is an example entry from this file:

```
<action name="jump" onPress="1" keyboard="space" xboxpad="xi_a"
  ps3pad="pad_cross"/>
```

In the preceding excerpt, an Action with the name `jump` is linked to three different input events, that is, it will trigger on either of them. It is mapped to the Space bar on the keyboard, the *A* button on the Xbox controller, and the *X* button on the PS3 controller. The entry also defined when the Action event should be sent out with the `onPress="1"` attribute. The exact syntax of an Action mapping is explained in detail in the section *Creating a new Action*.

Multiple Action Maps

If you take a closer look at the `defaultprofile.xml`, you will notice that there are several Action Maps contained within the file, each with a different name. This is no mistake; there is a very good reason for this.

In every game or simulation, the same key or button is commonly used for multiple actions. During gameplay, the *A* button on a controller might, for example, trigger a jump, but in a menu it would select an option on the interface. If the game has an inventory for the player, pressing *A* while it is open might select an item. And if the player is inside a vehicle, the *A* button could trigger the handbrake. Similar multiple assignments can be found for lots of other input events, especially since the number of buttons on a game controller is fairly limited.

To accommodate this, the `defaultprofile.xml` contains several entries that map the same button to various Action events. One example is the *A* button on the Xbox controller, which is represented by the keyword `xi_a`. This is mapped to the `jump` event as well as the vehicle brake `v_brake` and a range of menu actions. When this button is pressed, all these Action events might be triggered. Creating individual Action event entries for each of these actions is sensible, as it allows the player to customize their controls individually. The player might choose to keep the default assignment for jumping, but prefer the *B* button to be the handbrake inside vehicles. Splitting the actions up into separate events allows this kind of freedom.

But how can we prevent the code responsible for jumping from making the player jump while they are in a vehicle or while they are navigating their inventory or an in-game menu? Of course, the code could perform checks and only trigger the jump when none of these conditions apply. However, this would require an unnecessary amount of overhead as the code that should only be concerned with the player jumping now also needs to know about menus, inventories, and the vehicle system. The overhead code would get larger with each new system that reacted to inputs.

Instead, CryENGINE separates all Actions into multiple, separate Action Maps that can be individually activated or deactivated. Action events from an Action Map will only trigger if that map is currently active. For example, one Action Map would only handle the player inside a vehicle. It contains the mappings for all vehicle controls, such as acceleration and brakes. This Action Map is only activated once the player enters a vehicle (as a driver). The rest of the time it is disabled and none of the vehicle control Action events will trigger. The code handling the vehicle Actions would not need to perform any unnecessary checks. Accordingly, when a vehicle is entered, Action Maps to control swimming or player locomotion are disabled.

The CryENGINE SDK uses different Action Maps for various game modes, UI menus, different camera modes, singleplayer/multiplayer, and debug actions that are used only during project development. Some of Crytek's previously released games even used special Action Maps for some boss fights to change the controls as per the specific needs of the fight. Of course, more than one Action Map can be active at a time.

If you write a completely new system for your game project that comes with its own set of controls, you might consider creating an entirely new Action Map inside `defaultprofile.xml`. To do so, create a new `actionmap` tag node inside the XML file and then place your mapped actions inside as follows:

```
<actionmap name="newName">
  <action … />
  <action … />
  <action … />
</actionmap>
```

All maps will be automatically loaded, so you won't need to add any extra managing code for it. You can enable and disable your Action Map via the ActionMapManager inside your system, as shown in the following code:

```
#include <IActionMapManager.h>

// retrieve a pointer to the Action Map Manager
IActionMapManager* pActionMapMan = g_pGame->GetIGameFramework()-
>GetIActionMapManager();

// enable an Action Map
pActionMapMan->EnableActionMap("vehicle_general", true);

// disable an Action Map
pActionMapMan->EnableActionMap("player ", false);
```

The preceding sample code is written for use inside the CryGameSDK DLL, where the global variable g_pGame is defined. When working with ActionMaps, this is the DLL in which you will spend most of your time. If you are working with a full source code and want to access the ActionMapManager from there, use gEnv->pGame instead. Inside the CryAction DLL, you may also use CCryAction::GetCryAction()->GetIActionMapManager(); to retrieve the pointer to the ActionMapManager.

> Disabling an ActionMap is not the only way you can prevent certain Action events from triggering. You can also create specific Action filters. See the *Filtering Actions* section for more details.

Creating a new Action

The CryENGINE SDK is shipped with a large range of Actions already set up and implemented. Most of these Actions will be relevant to many types of games, such as player movement, shooting, weapon selection, and vehicle controls. While you will be keeping those in place, you will most certainly want to extend the system with your own Actions as well. This section will cover how to create a new Action in the Game Actions system and map input events to it.

There are two steps to setting up a new Action:

1. Create the new Action event.
2. Set up a mapping for it inside an ActionMap.

Setting up an Action event

To create a new Action event, you will need to create a new ActionId for it. This is basically just a string containing the name of the event and it is how Actions are referenced inside the codebase. To simplify the process for this, all Action events are listed in one file: GameActions.actions. This file is located inside the GameDll folder under GameSDK and is also included in the Visual Studio CryGameSDK project. This is an excerpt from this file:

```
DECL_ACTION(moveleft)
DECL_ACTION(moveright)
DECL_ACTION(moveforward)
DECL_ACTION(moveback)
DECL_ACTION(jump)
DECL_ACTION(crouch)
DECL_ACTION(sprint)
```

To add your own Action events, first choose an appropriate and descriptive name for your Action. It cannot contain whitespaces. Then, simply add it to the bottom of the file and surround your Action event with the DECL_ACTION() macro. This is defined in GameActions.h and the CGameActions class in this file creates ActionIds for all events listed in the GameActions.actions file. The new entry in the files could look something like this:

```
DECL_ACTION(your_new_action_name)
```

After you have added your Action in this file, you will need to recompile the CryGameSDK for both 64- and 32-bit before you can start using your new Action. But first you will need to map input events to it, which will be explained in the next section.

Adding an Action mapping

Once the Action event setup is done, you can add a mapping for your Action into one of the ActionMaps in the defaultprofile.xml file. You can create your own ActionMap of course, but keep in mind that you will also need to take care of activating and deactivating it. In most cases, you will be adding to the existing player ActionMap. This map is activated automatically at game start, so you will not need to add any extra managing code.

Names of ActionMaps sometimes change with new CryENGINE SDK releases. It is generally a good choice to add new player-related Actions into the map that also contain the regular player movement Actions, such as moveforward, moveleft, moveback, and moveright.

To add a new Action, open the `defaultprofile.xml` file from `Game/Libs/config` in a text editor. An editor that has syntax highlighting for a XML file is preferable, but not required. Since the file will be a few hundred lines long, the fastest way to find the ActionMap you want to modify is to do a quick search for its name, for example, `player`.

New Actions have to be added inside the tags for the ActionMap. Each ActionMap has an opening and a closing tag as shown in the following code snippet:

```
<actionmap name="player ">
...
<!-- New Actions go here, in between the actionmap tags -->
...
</action>
```

Each Action mapping gets its own XML entry, which has to be the tag `action`. There are a number of attributes that can be set on the node. Most are optional, but at the very least an entry has to have a name for the Action event it is supposed to trigger, one input event that is associated with it, and a trigger option.

```
<!-- Minimalistic Action mapping -->
<action name="jump" keyboard="space" onPress="1" />
```

To specify which input events will trigger the Action, you need to specify the device and the name of the input event. There are three devices: `xboxpad`, `ps3pad`, and `keyboard`. While the Xbox and PS3 controller are obvious, the `keyboard` attribute is used to access both the keyboard and the mouse input, although these are technically two devices. The distinction is made internally based upon the name of the events.

You can specify one, two, or all three devices inside the action node. You will need to decide which are relevant for the platform you are developing. The devices and their events can be set either as attributes or as children of the action node:

```
<action name="jump" keyboard="space" onPress="1" />
// The above entry creates the same mapping as the one below
<action name="jump" >
  <keyboard input="space" />
</action>
```

Using individual children rather than attributes inside the main action node allows you to bind more than one input event from the same device to an Action. This is especially useful for the *Enter* key that exists at two places on most standard keyboards (once on the main block, and once on the numeric keypad). Each of these keys generates an input event with a different name, yet it is expected that both keys work the same way, that is, they trigger the same Action. For example, if the *Enter* key would cause a dialog line to be skipped in your game, your players will most likely expect that the *Enter* key on the numeric keypad will have the same effect.

```
<action name="skip_dialogfragment" onPress="1" xboxpad="xi_b" >
  <keyboard>
    <inputdata input="enter"/>
    <inputdata input="np_enter"/>
  </keyboard>
</action>
```

The preceding action mapping example would link the Action of skipping of a dialog line to both *Enter* keys. Note that it also maps it to the *B* button on the Xbox controller. This is done inside the main `action` node. You can combine different input devices as attributes or children of the main action node.

In order to set up the appropriate input events inside the Action Map, you need to know their names. These are very straightforward for most keyboard keys, but not so for special keys such as the numeric keypad and function keys as well as the mouse and controller input events. You can find a table listing the most important input event names at the end of this chapter in the *The input event names reference* section.

Optional parameters

There are a number of optional attributes that can be set on an action node to further specify when and how the Action event is supposed to be triggered. These options will be explained in this section.

Trigger options

A trigger option defines when the Action event should be sent out if one of the mapped input events is received. In all the examples listed so far, the trigger option was set to `onPress="1"`, which will send the Action event once when the button or key is pressed down.

Keyboard keys and buttons on a mouse or a controller can trigger Actions when being pressed down, when they are released, and/or repeatedly while they are being held down. This is useful for many game mechanics. In a fighting game, for example, a player might have to press a key or button to enter a defensive block stance and then hold it to stay in that stance. He exits the stance as soon as he releases it again. In such a case, the Action would have the trigger options onPress and onRelease set up.

Attribute	Effect
onPress	This triggers the Action event once when the key/button is pressed down
onRelease	This triggers the Action event once when the key/button is released
onHold	This sends out the Action event repeatedly while the key/button is being held (see the following table for more parameters)

The preceding table lists the three available trigger options and describes their effects. You can set up more than one trigger option for an Action mapping. An entry in your Action Map could look like the following code:

```
<action name="jump" onPress="1" onRelease="1" keyboard="space"/>
```

You can also specify different trigger options for each device and input. For example, have the Action immediately triggered when the mapped key on the keyboard is pressed, but only trigger it on release of the mapped button on the Xbox controller. This is done using the following code snippet:

```
<action name="menu_open" >
  <keyboard input="x" onPress="1" />
  <xboxpad input="xi_back" onRelease="1" />
</action>
```

Each of the three trigger options onPress, onHold, and onRelease allow further parameters to be specified. All of these are optional and are not required for the option to work.

OnPress parameters

By default, the onPress option will trigger the Action event immediately when the input event is received. However, this behavior can be altered and the event can be delayed. The following table lists the additional attributes you can specify. These must be set on the same node as the onPress attribute:

Attribute	Effect
pressTriggerDelay	This specifies the delay (in seconds) before the Action event is triggered after the key or button was pressed.
pressDelayPriority	This specifies that only one Action can be delayed at a time. If another delayed Action is triggered before this one has fired, the one with the lower delay priority will be discarded.
pressTriggerDelayRepeatOverride	If this is set set to 1, pressing the same key again will abort the delay timer and trigger the event immediately. If it is set to 0, pressing the key again will restart the delay timer.

If the onPress trigger is delayed, then onRelease will be delayed as well automatically. It will not trigger until the onPress has triggered. This ensures that the onPress and the onRelease events are always triggered in their logical order.

OnHold parameters

When the option onHold is specified, the Game Action system will repeatedly trigger the mapped Action event while the key or button is being held down. This option allows further parameters to set the frequency of the events and an initial delay.

A delay is a length of time between the initial key press and before the repeated Action events are being triggered. You can easily visualize what this means by opening a text editor and holding down a letter key on your keyboard. After typing the letter once, there will be a short delay before your screen will start filling up.

The onHold parameters are specified as attributes in the same XML node where the onHold attribute is set. Here is an example setup:

```
<action name="menu_up" onHold="1" holdTriggerDelay="0.5"
holdRepeatDelay="0.15" >
  <keyboard input="up" />
</action>
```

When specifying onHold inside an action tag, you will usually want to also specify one or more parameters to configure the trigger option. The following table lists the available parameters:

Attribute	Effect
holdTriggerDelay	This specifies the delay (in seconds) after pressing before the first Action event is triggered.
holdRepeatDelay	This specifies the time (in seconds) between individual Action events. The -1 value will only trigger once after pressing and there will be no repeats.

 The onHold trigger is commonly specified together with the onPress trigger option.

OnRelease parameters

Unlike the other two trigger options, onRelease does not have its own delay parameter. However, as mentioned in the description of the onPress trigger option, the onRelease trigger will be delayed automatically in case the onPress trigger is delayed.

This ensures that the events are always being triggered in order. However, it is possible to prevent onRelease to trigger the Action event altogether if a certain amount of time has passed since the key or button was pressed, or in other words, a trigger timeout.

This is done with the releaseTriggerThreshold attribute. Like the other parameters, it needs to be set in the same node as the onRelease option. The following is an example of how to use this parameter:

```
<action name="detonate" onRelease="1" releaseTriggerThreshold="3">
  <keyboard input="h" />
</action>
```

With the preceding setup, the detonate Action will only trigger if the h key was pressed and released, but only if the key was not held down for more than 3 seconds.

Analog input

A key on a keyboard or a button on a mouse only has two states it can be in, either up or down. The Xbox and PS3 game controllers, however, also have analog controls such as the thumb sticks and the trigger buttons. These controls have no distinct pressed/released states, but instead deliver a value that represents how far they are pressed or how far they have been moved from the center.

You can access the analog value of these inputs in the code that will react to the Action event and use them to modify the game mechanics. The mapping in the ActionMaps also allows us to do some preprocessing of these values.

By using the parameters for analog input handling, you can prevent the Action event from being triggered unless the thumb stick or trigger button are moved above a specified threshold. The following table explains the three attributes required for this. All three need to be specified if analog preprocessing is to be used.

Mode	Effect
useAnalogCompare	This is set to 1 to enable analog pre processing.
analogCompareVal	This is the floating point value to compare the analog value against.
analogCompareOp	This is the operator to use with the compare value mode. Possible values are: EQUALS, NOTEQUALS, GREATERTHAN and LESSTHAN.

Modifiers

By default, holding *Shift*, *Alt*, *Ctrl*, or the Windows key while pressing any key on the keyboard will be ignored. For example, an Action linked to the input event h will trigger even if the *Shift* key is held, making the input into a capital letter H.

By specifying noModifiers="1" as an attribute, the Action requires that neither of these modifier keys must be pressed for the event to trigger. In the preceding example, the Action would not trigger when *H* is typed.

> The keyboard input events are case-insensitive. Specifying the input event h in an Action mapping has the same result as specifying H in the mapping.

Triggering console commands

During development, it is often necessary to assign a number of debug keys to help with testing and debugging. These inputs can be assigned a range of different functionality, but one common purpose is to trigger console commands in the debug console. To make the development process easier, Action Maps allow input events to trigger console commands directly, without the need to create handling code or FlowGraphs.

The following Action mapping demonstrates how this can be set up. You will need to specify `consoleCmd="1"` to indicate that this Action is a direct console command. The string inside the attribute `name` will be executed in the console. You can use this to set console variables or call console commands with parameters.

```
<action consoleCmd="1" keyboard="f5" name="save" onPress="1" />
```

This functionality is mainly used to perform debugging and testing; but in the preceding example of `QuickSave`, it can even be used as a game feature.

Reacting to Action events

Now that you have one or multiple new Action events set up and input events mapped to them, you need to learn how to listen to the Action so that you can respond to it when it is triggered. You can do this in code or in the FlowGraph.

Action events in code

When reacting to Actions, you can either set up your own class to receive the Action events, or you can extend the main existing Action event handler inside `PlayerInput.cpp`. The next section will cover how to set up a new Action event listener from scratch. This can be useful if, for example, you are implementing a new FlowGraph node that is supposed to trigger when receiving specific Action events. In most cases, however, adding handler code for new Actions inside the `PlayerInput` class is sufficient. Also, it is both faster and more convenient than setting up an entirely new listener. So, feel free to skip ahead to the *Extending PlayerInput* section at this time.

Setting up a new Action listener

The Game Action system is implemented like a regular event system. This means it has a list of listener classes that it manages internally whenever an event is triggered, a callback function is called in every class in that list with the event name and some parameters. In order for any class to receive the events it sends out, it needs to derive from a listener interface base class and register itself with the system as a listener.

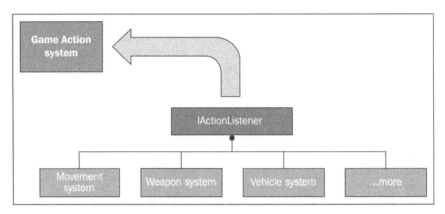

Classes need to derive from the IActionListener interface to receive Action events

Note that the preceding diagram is only for demonstration. In fact, most classes are actually not derived from the IActionListener interface directly. They either receive their triggers via the PlayerInput class or are implemented as GameObject, which is in turn derived from the IActionListener interface.

For the Game Action system, the interface class that you will need to derive your system from is called IActionListener. This is defined in the file IActionMapManager.h, which you will need to include in your own header file as follows:

```
#include <IActionMapManager.h>

class CMyOwnClass : public IActionListener
{
public:
  // ...
};
```

After deriving from the interface, you will need to implement the callback function to receive the Action events. This function is called `OnAction` and should be declared as follows:

```
virtual void OnAction(const ActionId& action, int activationMode,
float value) {}
```

You can leave the body of the function empty for now. Before you can start catching the event, you will need to register your class as a listener with the ActionMapManager. Inside your classes initialization function, add the following lines of code:

```
IGameFramework* pGameFrmWk = gEnv->pGame->GetIGameFramework();
IActionMapManager* pActMan = pGameFrmWk->GetIActionMapManager();
pActMan->AddExtraActionListener(this);
```

Now, your `OnAction()` function will be called whenever an Action event is being triggered. The parameters of this function are practically the same as they were for the handler functions when extending the PlayerInput class, so please see the next section for a detailed description.

Extending PlayerInput

The class `CPlayerInput` inside `PlayerInput.cpp` in the Game DLL handles almost all Action events that are related to the player. The player class `CPlayer` itself is implemented as a `GameObject` (meaning it has a `GameObject` proxy), which is derived from the `IActionListener` interface. The `CPlayerInput` class registers itself with the player's `GameObject` as the main Action handler class. This means the `GameObject` will forward all received Action events to this class.

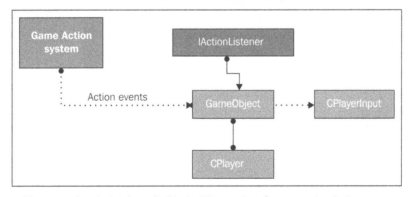

Classes need to derive from the IActionListener interface to receive Action events

The `CPlayerInput` class links a list of handler functions to specific Action events. If the class receives a certain Action event, it will call the linked function automatically.

It is very easy to add your own handler code in this class. For one, it is good practice to keep all code related to input inside one class, as it makes debugging simpler. But it also requires the least amount of work, since you don't need to write any management code to register or deregister yourself from the `ActionMapManager`. All you need to add is one function to handle the specific Action event that you are interested in and a single line to register it inside `CPlayerInput`.

Creating a new handler function

To add a handler for your newly created Action, implement a new function inside the `CPlayerInput` class. The function needs to follow a specific declaration:

```
bool NewHandlerFunction(EntityId entityId, const ActionId&
    actionId, int activationMode, float value);
```

Let's take a look at the parameters of this function. The first parameter is the entity ID of the player character. The second parameter is the name of the Action event. As your handler function will be linked directly to just one Action, this is irrelevant at this point. If you are implementing an Action listener from scratch or are using the same handler function for more than one Action event, you can use this variable to distinguish between different Actions.

The third parameter, `activationMode`, contains the trigger options that spawned the event. This will correspond to the trigger options set up in the mapping, and the values are either `eAAM_OnPress`, `eAAM_OnRelease`, or `eAAM_OnHold`.

The last parameter, `value`, contains an analog value. What this value represents depends on the input device. For keyboard keys and mouse buttons, this value will either be 0 or 1. However, for game controllers' thumb sticks or trigger buttons, this represents how far the trigger or stick is pushed. For mouse movements and the mouse wheel, this contains a delta value.

You can use these values to modify your response to the Action event. The intensity with which a trigger button is pressed determines how fast a vehicle is accelerates. Otherwise, the distance of the thumb stick from the center determines whether the player is walking or running.

When working with these values, consider that due to the nature of analog sticks these hardly ever return to an exact 0.0 value when they are released. It might make sense to work with a so-called "dead zone", which is a small range around 0.0 in which your function simply ignores the Action and pretends the stick was at the center. This way you will prevent things like camera or player movement when the user is not even touching the thumb stick.

When you implement your handler function inside the source file, be sure to return `true` to indicate that you have handled the event.

Registering your handler function

Before your handler function will be called, you will need to link it to the Action event you want it to handle. This is done in a single line in the CPlayerInput's constructor. All handler functions are registered here. This is an excerpt from the constructor:

```
ADD_HANDLER(moveforward, OnActionMoveForward);
ADD_HANDLER(moveback, OnActionMoveBack);
ADD_HANDLER(moveleft, OnActionMoveLeft);
ADD_HANDLER(moveright, OnActionMoveRight);
```

The `ADD_HANDLER` function has two parameters: the name of the Action event you intend to handle and the function that handles it. At the bottom of the constructor, add your own function and Action event.

```
ADD_HANDLER(NewAction, NewHandlerFunction);
```

Now, you are all set to receive Action events and respond to them.

Custom Action Maps

If you are using your own custom ActionMaps and want to extend the `CPlayerInput` class, you will need to complete an additional step in order to receive the events from your Action Map. This step is not required if you implemented your own `IActionListener` interface from scratch.

Each ActionMap internally stores an `EntityId`. When an Action event is triggered it is passed into the corresponding `GameObject`. This is how `CPlayerInput` receives its callbacks. So, the new Action Map must be told the `EntityId` of the player so that the `PlayerInput` will be able to handle its Action events.

If you have full source access, you can put this code inside the file `CET_ActionMap.cpp` inside CryAction, where most ActionMaps are enabled and set up. Otherwise, place it somewhere inside the `CryGameSDK` DLL, possibly inside the `Reset()` function in `PlayerInput.cpp` if you would like to keep all input related code in one place.

```
IGameFramework* pGameFrmWk = gEnv->pGame->GetIGameFramework();
IActionMapManager* pActMan = pGameFrmWk->GetIActionMapManager();
IActionMap* pActnMap = pActMan->GetActionMap("NewActionMap");
pActnMap->SetActionListener( m_pPlayer->GetEntityId() );
```

At times, during development, keys are mapped to help with debugging and QA testing. They can allow the developer to quickly jump to certain locations, trigger events, cut scene, give inventory items, ammo, and so on.

It can be helpful to gather all these debug mappings inside a debug Action Map. Then, simply remove or deactivate this Action Map before shipping. This way you won't need to remove the code for it and risk breaking your build in the process, but you also don't have to worry about players using your debug keys to cheat.

Action events in FlowGraph

You don't need to meddle with the source code to react to Action events. The FlowGraph node **Input:Action** offers easy access to the Game Actions system. To use this node, you will only need to know the name of the Action you want to respond to and the ActionMap it is defined in.

Inside your FlowGraph, add the node **Input:Action**. The node can only react to onPress and onRelease triggers; the onHold trigger will be ignored. The node looks like the following:

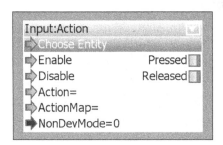

Before you can use this node, you will need to set up your Action event and ActionMap name. The node also requires the local player's entity to be assigned on it. You will also need to call the **Enable** port once to start listening to events. A possible setup can look like the following:

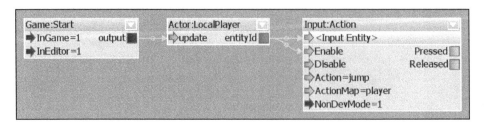

Generally, it is recommended that you don't use this FlowGraph node to listen to Action events, because the current implementation does not make use of the Game Actions system properly. It neither checks whether an ActionMap is active or not, nor does it respect the trigger options. If you need a proper Action event listening FlowGraph node for your project, you can use the information in this chapter to implement your own.

The **Input:Action** node is mostly used during development for debugging and testing purposes. By default, it will not work in the launcher. You will need to enable the **NonDevMode** checkbox if you want it to work in the launcher.

Filtering Actions

As mentioned before, it is possible to enable and disable entire Action Maps completely and block their Action events from triggering. This is useful for segments of the game when the controls need to change completely, such as if the player entered a vehicle or is currently in the pause menu.

However, sometimes it can become necessary to only prevent certain Action events from triggering, while leaving the rest of the ActionMap intact. The most common use case, for example, is when the player's movement is restricted. If the player is currently balancing over a broken tree or climbing a wall, they might still be able to move forward and backwards, but not left or right. Also, they might still be allowed to fire their weapon, but not enter crouch mode. Another common example is turret gameplay, where the player's movement is completely blocked, but their rotation or their ability to fire is not.

In these cases, instead of switching to an entirely new ActionMap completely, you can choose to temporarily filter out the unwanted Actions. This is done using **Action Filters**.

Creating Action Filters

Action Filters are created in code, and they need to be registered with the ActionMapManager. The best place to do this is inside the CGameActions class in GameActions.h/GameActions.cpp. This class has direct access to all registered Action events and it is accessible from the CryGameSDK DLL. If you register your filter from another place, you should include GameActions.h and refer to the Action events by using CGameAction::ActionEventName. This section will take you through the process of creating a new Action Filter.

First, you need to retrieve a pointer to the ActionMapManager. Then you can create a new Action Filter. You will need to provide a name for the filter to access it again later and a filtering mode. There are two modes available:

Mode	Effect
eAFT_ActionPass	Only Action events of this type are allowed to trigger while this filter is active
eAFT_ActionFail	Action events of this type are blocked while the filter is active, all others are allowed

Then, you can start adding Actions to the newly created filter. Here is some example code that creates a simple filter to block player movement:

```
IGameFramework* pGameFrmWk = gEnv->pGame->GetIGameFramework();
IActionMapManager* pActMan = pGameFrmWk->GetIActionMapManager();

IActionFilter* pNewFilter;
pNewFilter = pActMan ->CreateActionFilter("no_move", eAFT_ActionFail);
pNewFilter->Filter(jump);
pNewFilter->Filter(moveleft);
pNewFilter->Filter(moveright);
pNewFilter->Filter(moveforward);
pNewFilter->Filter(moveback);
```

Using Action Filters

Once the Action Filter has been created, it can be activated or deactivated either from code or from FlowGraph. Both mechanics are explained as follows:

- To enable a filter via code, you have two options. You can call the filter directly, provided you have a pointer to it, for example if you stored it after creation. Alternatively, you can use the ActionMapManager to access a filter via its name. Here are the functions at your disposal:

```
IActionMapManager::EnableFilter(const char *name, bool
  enable)
IActionFilter::Enable(bool enable)
```

- In FlowGraph, you can enable or disable the filters via the node **Actor:ActionFilter**. (This node was called **Input:ActionFilter** in the previous releases of CryENGINE.) Like the **Input:Action** node, it requires the local player's entity to be set on the node in order to work. Here is how a setup with the **no_move** filter created in the previous section could look:

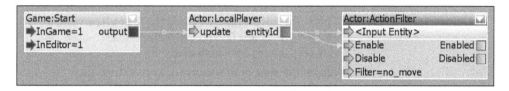

Reacting to Input events

Up to this point, Action events have been covered quite extensively as a layer of abstraction on top of the input system. In general, Actions are preferable to the raw input events due to the many advantages of Actions.

It is also possible to listen and react to input events from CryInput directly. This section will also cover how to listen and respond to these events in code and in the FlowGraph.

Code

Like the Game Actions system, the input system is an event system. It sends out the input events to all classes that have registered themselves as listeners. To become a listener, a class needs to derive from the interface `IInputEventListener`.

```
#include <IInput.h>

class CMyOwnClass : public IInputEventListener
{
public:
  // ...
};
```

To compile this without error, the class needs to implement the callback function that the input system will call with the input events. This function should return `false` to allow other listeners to also receive the event. If `true` is returned, the rest of the listeners will not be called.

```
virtual bool OnInputEvent( const SInputEvent &event );
```

This function will receive all input events dispatched by the input system, coming from all supported devices. The parameter event contains all information about the input event needed to process it. These are the members of the `SInputEvent` struct and their descriptions:

Member	Effect
deviceId	This is the device that triggered the event. The values are eDI_Keyboard (keyboard), eDI_Mouse (mouse), and eDI_XI (Xbox or PS3 controller).
state	This is the state of the button or key. Values are eIS_Pressed (key/button was pressed), eIS_Released (key/button was released), eIS_Down (key/button is held down), and eIS_Changed (changed state (toggle controls)).
keyName	This is the name of the input event. See the input name reference table at the end of the chapter.
keyId	This is the enum identifier of the input event. As an optimization, instead of comparing strings with the keyName, you can compare keyId, using the EKeyId enum in IInput.h.
modifiers	These are the key modifiers enabled at the time of this event. This is an integer value comprised of any combination of these flags: eMM_Ctrl, eMM_Shift, eMM_Alt, and eMM_Win.
value	This is the analog value associated with the event. See the section *Creating a new handler function*.
pSymbol	This is the type of control that created the input event: Button, Toggle, RawAxis, Axis, and Trigger.
deviceIndex	This is the controller index, in case there are multiple. This can be important on consoles.

Most key and button presses will trigger at least two input events: once when the key is pressed down and once again when it is released. A common implementation of the `OnInputEvent()` function compares the `keyName` to all input event names it wants to react to, and then it checks the state of the input control before it reacts to the input. The state check is necessary so that the code doesn't respond to the same key pressed twice. This is not necessary of course for the non-button events, such as the mouse wheel or mouse movement for example.

You can either check the `keyName` directly by using a string compare or check the `keyId` against the enum value of your input event. A table listing the most common input event names can be found at the end of this chapter in the section *The input event names reference*.

FlowGraph

The FlowGraph also provides the option to react to input events, making it easy for level designers to prototype new ideas. The node for this is called **Debug:InputKey** (note that this was called **Input:Key** in the previous CryENGINE releases).

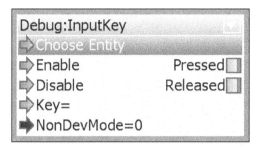

Having many of these nodes in a level will cause a lot of string compare operations in nearly every frame, which can take a bite out of performance. In addition to that, input events are not filtered (like Action events), nor can they be remapped easily at runtime. Therefore, it is advised that all functionality prototyped with this node should be converted into a code-based solution. Instead of input events, it would also make sense to use Actions in this implementation.

To encourage implementing Actions properly, this node has been moved into the **Debug** category by Crytek. This means it is not intended to be used in a shipped product, but only for development and debugging purposes. By default, it will not work outside of the Sandbox editor.

To make this node work in launcher, it must have the local player's entity assigned to it, the **NonDevMode** checkbox must be checked, and the **Enable** port has to be triggered. Depending on your system configuration, you might also need to set the console variable `g_disableInputKeyFlowNodeInDevMode` to `0` inside your `system.cfg` file.

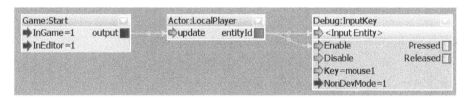

The preceding example shows how to receive left and right mouse movements by using the **Debug:InputKey** FlowGraph node. To catch input events with this node, you need to provide the name of the input event in the **Key** port of the node. A table listing the most common input event names can be found at the end of this chapter in the section *The input event names reference*.

User profiles

One of the distinct advantages of using Action Maps instead of input events is the ability to allow the player to customize the input controls of the game to their personal preferences. The modified Action Maps are saved and loaded using user profiles.

This section will explain how to modify an ActionMap at runtime as well as how to load and save them. You will need to decide whether adding this functionality makes sense for your type of project.

> Apart from the Action mapping, user profiles also store a list of personal settings, such as brightness, volume, and difficulty level. As these are not input system relevant, they will not be covered in this chapter. If you want to learn more, please take a look at the `attributes.xml` file at Game\Libs\Config\Profiles\default.

Modifying user profiles

User profiles are managed inside the `CryAction` DLL, but they can be accessed and modified from anywhere in the codebase. Full source access is not required. If you want to allow players to change the controller mappings in your game, you would offer a menu of some kind. Once you know which Action you want to remap to which input events, you can access the user profile and modify it.

To access the user profile you need to use the `PlayerProfileManager`, which you can retrieve from the `GameFramework`. If you like, you can put your code into the `CGame` class inside `Game.cpp`, as it already includes all the necessary header file to work with profiles as seen in the following code snippet:

```
#include <IPlayerProfiles.h>
IPlayerProfileManager* pProfileMgr =
  gEnv->pGame->GetIGameFramework()->GetIPlayerProfileManager();
```

The profile manager lets you access the currently active profile. For this, you will need the username of the user that is currently logged into the system on which your game is running. On a Windows machine, this will be the username that was used to log in; on a console such as the Xbox, this is the name of the user currently signed in to the system. Most platforms support multiple users, and CryENGINE manages separate profiles for each of them.

```
const char* userName = pProfileMgr->GetCurrentUser();
IPlayerProfile* pProfile =
    pProfileMgr->GetCurrentProfile(userName);
```

Once you have a pointer to the current profile, you can retrieve an ActionMap by its name and rebind an Action to a different input event. This is the function to change the mapping:

```
virtual bool ReBindActionInput(const ActionId& actionId,
      const char* szCurrentInput,
      const char* szNewInput);
```

The first parameter asks for the ActionId of the Action you wish to change. You will need to include the file GameActions.h to access the ActionIds as they were declared in the GameActions.actions file (see the section *Setting up an Action event*). Next, you will need the names of the input events this Action is currently bound to and the one to which you want to change the mapping.

```
#include "GameActions.h"

pProfile->GetActionMap("player")->ReBindActionInput(g_pGameActions-
>jump, "space", "k");
```

Since there can be more than one input event mapped to one Action event, you will need to specify which one you intend to change. The preceding example rebinds the jump Action from the Space bar to the letter k. The Action is also bound to the *A* button on the Xbox controller. This mapping, however, was unchanged.

After you changed a user profile, you need to save it again so that the changes are not lost once the game is quit. You can do so by telling the profile manager to save out the profile currently active for this user as follows:

```
IPlayerProfileManager::EProfileOperationResult profileResult;
pProfileMgr ->SaveProfile(username, profileResult, ePR_All);
```

User profiles are stored inside the PROFILENAME folder under USER\Profiles, which is created in the build's root folder when CryENGINE is started for the first time. You can navigate there in a file explorer and look at the content. The XML files are stored in binary format, however, and cannot be edited with a text editor.

All available profiles are automatically scanned at the start of the game, so you don't need to manually load them. To switch to a different profile, simply activate it in the profile manager as follows:

```
pProfileMgr ->ActivateProfile(userName, profileName);
```

DLCs and patches

Note that when you save the Action mapping in the user profile, only the mappings that differ from the default profile are being stored. If you release a patch for your game at a later time with some changed or added Action mappings, the `defaultprofile.xml` file will work as expected.

In case you want to force the player to use your updated mapping with a patch or DLC and discard previously modified Action Maps, you can increase the version number at the top of the `defaultprofile.xml` file. If the version number in there is larger than the one stored in the user profile, the player-modified map will be ignored.

The input event names reference

A list of the most common CryENGINE input event names (as used inside ActionMaps, FlowGraph nodes, and input event listeners in code) is given in this section.

Keyboard

The following table shows the input event names for the keyboard:

Key	Input event name
Esc	`"escape"`
-	`"minus"`
- (numpad)	`"no_subtract"`
=	`"equals"`
Backspace	`"backspace"`
Tab	`"tab"`
(	`"lbracket"`
)	`"rbracket"`
Enter	`"enter"`
Enter (numpad)	`"np_enter"`
Ctrl (left)	`"lctrl"`
Ctrl (right)	`"rctrl"`

Key	Input event name
;	`"semicolon"`
:	`"colon"`
'	`"apostrophe"`
~	`"tilde"`
Shift (left)	`"lshift"`
Shift (right)	`"rshift"`
\	`"backslash"`
,	`"comma"`
.	`"period"`
. (numpad)	`"np_period"`
/	`"slash"`
/ (numpad)	`"np_divide"`
* (numpad)	`"np_multiply"`
_	`"underline"`
Alt (left)	`"lalt"`
Alt (right)	`"ralt"`
Space bar	`"space"`
Caps Lock	`"capslock"`
Function keys *F1 - F12*	`"f1"` to `"f12"`
Num Lock	`"numlock"`
Scroll Lock	`"scrolllock"`
Numpad *0 - 9*	`"np_0"` to `"np_9"`
+ (numpad)	`"np_add"`
Print Screen	`"print"`
Pause/Break	`"pause"`
Home	`"home"`
Up arrow	`"up"`
Left arrow	`"left"`
Right arrow	`"right"`
Down arrow	`"down"`
Page Up	`"pgup"`
Page Down	`"pgdn"`
End	`"end"`
Insert	`"insert"`
Delete	`"delete"`

Mouse

The following table shows the input event names for the mouse:

Mouse event	Input event name
Left mouse button	`"mouse1"`
Right mouse button	`"mouse2"`
Middle mouse button	`"mouse3"`
Mouse wheel up	`"mwheel_up"`
Mouse wheel down	`"mwheel_down"`
Left/right mouse movement	`"maxis_x"`
Up/down mouse movement	`"maxis_y"`

Xbox 360 controller

The following table shows the input event names for the Xbox 360 controller:

Stick/Button	Input event name
D-pad up	`"xi_dpad_up"`
D-pad left	`"xi_dpad_left"`
D-pad right	`"xi_dpad_right"`
D-pad down	`"xi_dpad_down"`
Start button	`"xi_start"`
Select button	`"xi_back"`
Left shoulder button	`"xi_shoulderl"`
Left trigger button	`"xi_triggerl"`
Right shoulder button	`"xi_shoulderr"`
Right trigger button	`"xi_triggerr"`
A, B, X, and Y buttons	`"xi_a"`, `"xi_b"`, `"xi_x"`, and `"xi_y"`
Left thumb stick left/right	`"xi_thumblx"`
Left thumb stick up/down	`"xi_thumbly"`
Right thumb stick left/right	`"xi_thumbrx"`
Right thumb stick up/down	`"xi_thumbry"`
Pressing left thumb stick	`"xi_thumbl"`
Pressing right thumb stick	`"xi_thumbr"`

Stick/Button	Input event name
Left thumb stick movement	`"xi_thumbl_up"`, `"xi_thumbl_down"`, `"xi_thumbl_left"`, and `"xi_thumbl_right"`
Right thumb stick movement	`"xi_thumbr_up"`, `"xi_thumbr_down"`, `"xi_thumbr_left"` and `"xi_thumbr_right"`

PS3 controller

The following table shows the input event names for the PS3 controller:

Stick/button	Input event name
Select button	`"pad_select"`
Start button	`"pad_start"`
× button	`"pad_cross"`
□ button	`"pad_square"`
○ button	`"pad_circle"`
Δ button	`"pad_triangle"`
Left stick left/right	`"pad_sticklx"`
Left stick up/down	`"pad_stickly"`
Right stick left/right	`"pad_stickrx"`
Right stick up/down	`"pad_stickry"`
L1 button	`"pad_l1"`
L2 button	`"pad_l2"`
R1 button	`"pad_r1"`
R2 button	`"pad_r2"`
D-pad up	`"pad_up"`
D-pad left	`"pad_left"`
D-pad right	`"pad_right"`
D-pad down	`"pad_down"`

Summary

This chapter focused on the input system of CryENGINE. It detailed which input devices are currently supported and which part of the engine handles the communication with their hardware and drivers.

You learned about the different layers of abstraction, the input event system, about the Game Action system offer, and how this abstraction can benefit you in the development of your game.

With the code and FlowGraph examples in this chapter, you will be able to create your own game mechanics that react to Action and input events, as well as set up debugging keys that can boost your production speed.

The next chapter will introduce you to the some advanced features of the FlowGraph system, such as graph tokens and nested FlowGraphs.

3

Building Complex Flow Graph Logic

The flow graph is a visual scripting tool integrated into the CryENGINE Sandbox. It was first introduced in the engine with CryENGINE Version 2.0 and has since become one of the most important tools available to level and game designers to set up game logic.

The goal of this chapter is to learn about the more advanced techniques used when building CryENGINE flow graphs. We will look at complex flow graph setups using elements such as graph tokens, game tokens, and dynamic EntityId inputs.

Who uses the flow graph system?

The flow graph system allows designers and other nontechnical developers to set up complex game logic without touching any Lua or C++ code. You can use the flow graph system in many ways for your game production. You can use the flow graph to varying extents depending on the type of game you are working on. You can create a majority of your gameplay using the flow graph or maybe control only some simple gameplay elements of a level now and then. The flow graph can help you reduce your script writing. A huge library of flow graph nodes will save you a lot of scripting work. Depending on your role in production, you may have already used the flow graph to create game logic, build a user interface flow, or even to create AI actions and behaviors. In the next pages, we will go beyond this basic usage with the goal to fully utilize all the elements of the flow graph system.

A more complex application of the flow graph

In this chapter, we will not focus so much on the basics of the flow graph, but rather on the lesser known features and more complex applications of the system. At the beginner's level, flow graphs are generally created on an entity residing in the level. Then, entities usually existing in the level are used and connected using a set of component nodes. While these basic functionalities are great and already provide you with a lot of possibilities to script your gameplay, the true power of the flow graph only starts to show when working with dynamic EntityIDs, game tokens, and other advanced features.

Revisiting the basics of flow graphs

Let us quickly revisit the most important aspects of the flow graph system before we start getting into the more complex examples.

Types of nodes

All the flow graph nodes have input and output ports, which can be connected with links to trigger the functionalities of the nodes. A flow graph node can belong to one of two categories. A node is either an entity node or a component node. Although they may look quite similar, these two types of nodes function very differently.

Entity nodes

An entity node is a representation of an existing entity inside the flow graph. Most entities that have been placed in your CryENGINE level can be inserted into the flow graph as an entity node. This will give you access to all exposed functionalities of the entity.

The entity nodes can simply be created by opening the context menu in the flow graph and clicking on **Add Selected Entity**. An entity node placed this way will only function as long as the actual entity it is referring to still exists in the level. If the entity that the node is referring to is deleted, the entity node will stop working properly.

The **ProximityTrigger** entity shown in the following screenshot is a good example of how a basic entity node looks:

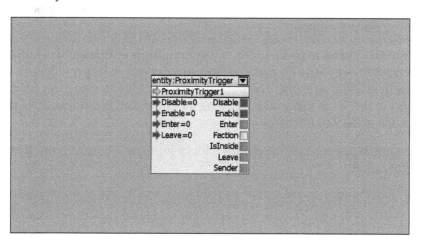

Component nodes

The second type of node, the component node, performs a certain action or behavior with no direct relation to an existing entity. There are many different component nodes with very different functionalities. While some might need an existing entity to work properly, others might just work independently without any connection to an entity. One of the most simple nodes in the flow graph, for example, is the **Misc:Start** node as shown in the following screenshot:

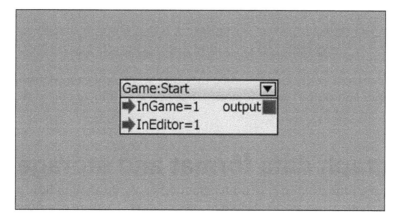

All this node does is output a signal once the game has started. It does not have any connection to any entity existing in the level. Nevertheless, it is extremely useful since it can be used to trigger all kinds of initializations, which are supposed to happen at the start of a game.

Other component nodes might use one or even multiple entities to work properly. The **Movement:MoveEntityTo** node, for example, needs to be provided an EntityId and a position in order to work. The purpose of the node is to move an entity to a certain point in the level. Without specifying an entity and providing a 3D position to move to, the node will not work.

The **Movement:MoveEntityTo** node has a lot of input and output ports that allow easy customization:

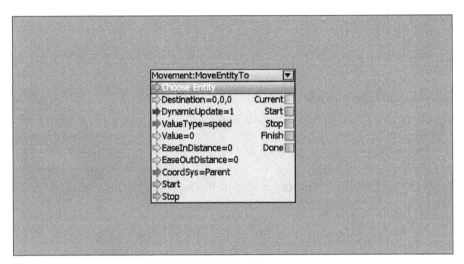

The Movement:MoveEntityTo node is a component node

Both component and entity nodes can be modified relatively easy. Adding or removing input and output ports to nodes is simple and allows you to tweak existing nodes to fit your needs.

Flow graph data format and storage

One of the more difficult things to understand when working with flow graphs is the way they are created and stored. While the actual data structure of a flow graph is relatively simple, understanding the way it is stored can be a bit more difficult.

Let's first have a look at how the data format of the flow graph looks. A rather simple flow graph should suffice for this example as shown in the following screenshot:

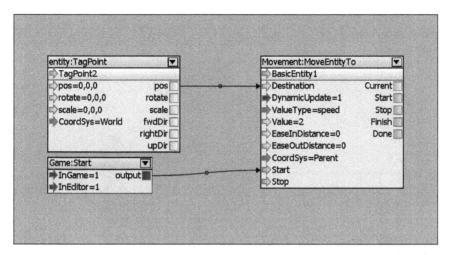

In order to look at the flow graph data format you need to create a simple example flow graph. The flow graph depicted in the preceding screenshot uses a **Misc:Start** node to trigger a **Movement:MoveEntityTo** node, which then moves an entity to the position of a tag point.

Let's build this flow graph and then export it to an XML file by performing the following steps:

1. Open the flow graph window and build the example flow graph as shown in the preceding screenshot.
2. Select all the nodes of your flow graph.
3. Select the selection/export option from the context menu to save the flow graph to your game folder.
4. Use Notepad++ or any other text editor to open the exported flow graph.

You just created and exported a simple flow graph. Now let's have a look at the exported file shown as follows:

```
<Graph Description="" Group="Main">
  <Nodes>
    <Node Id="26" Class="Game:Start" pos="-200,720,0" flags="1">
      <Inputs InGame="1" InEditor="1"/>
  </Node>
    <Node Id="27" Class="Movement:MoveEntityTo" pos="60,600,0"
```

```
        flags="1" EntityGUID="{66D6738E-E49F-4293-86AA-D05AE45212BB}"
          EntityGUID_64="4293E49F66D6738E">
        <Inputs entityId="0" Destination="0,0,0" DynamicUpdate="1"
          ValueType="0" Speed="2" EaseDistance="0" EaseOutDistance="0"
          CoordSys="0"/>
      </Node>
        <Node Id="29" Class="entity:TagPoint" pos="-200,600,0"
          flags="1" EntityGUID="{214E41E2-EB74-4498-A2EF-
          061DFDA7C070}" EntityGUID_64="4498EB74214E41E2">
        <Inputs entityId="0" pos="0,0,0" rotate="0,0,0" scale="0,0,0"
          CoordSys="1"/>
        </Node>
      </Nodes>
      <Edges>
        <Edge nodeIn="27" nodeOut="26" portIn="Start" portOut="output"
          enabled="1"/>
        <Edge nodeIn="27" nodeOut="29" portIn="Destination"
          portOut="pos" enabled="1"/>
      </Edges>
    </Graph>
```

Not too complex, is it? As you can see, the content of a flow graph is saved in a pretty straightforward XML format.

A node is identified with its Id and position coordinates, which tell the system where the node is located on the flow graph canvas. Additionally, an engine GUID is assigned, which helps the engine identify the flow graph node.

Let's take the section containing the **Misc:Start** node as an example. Its code snippet looks as follows:

```
<Nodes>
  <Node Id="26" Class="Game:Start" pos="-200,720,0" flags="1">
    <Inputs InGame="1" InEditor="1"/>
  </Node>
```

In the Edges section in the XML file, we can see each link of the node defined:

```
<Edges>
  <Edge nodeIn="27" nodeOut="26" portIn="Start" portOut="output"
    enabled="1"/>
```

The node with the Id value of 26 is connected to the node with the Id value of 27 using the ports called output and Start.

Looking at the simplicity of this structure, you could even edit your flow graphs manually using a text editor. For regular production, this is impractical of course. However, it is good to remember that in emergency situations, you can still fix or disable a certain flow graph without having access to the actual level.

In emergency situations, such as last-minute bugs before an important demonstration, which leave us with no chance to open the Sandbox flow graphs, they can be changed and repaired by directly editing the XML data using a text editor (without using Sandbox).

But where is this XML data actually saved when you just save your level in Sandbox? In your production environment, you will mostly just save your level to save your flow graphs. You will also usually only export a flow graph when you want to share it with somebody who has no access to your level.

Flow graphs are saved in your level as part of an entity. This means that when you save the entity, you also save the flow graph that belongs to it. Flow graphs can never exist as their own entity; they are always part of an entity existing somewhere in your level.

Flow graphs are always saved with the entity they have been created on. Once the entity is deleted, the flow graph will be lost.

At first, the procedure of creating and storing a flow graph as part of an entity may seem unnecessarily complicated, but it comes with a lot of advantages. For example, could a flow graph be shared or transferred to another level by importing the entity it belongs to? Alternatively, you could add an entity with a flow graph to a prefab and reuse it in other levels. Furthermore, since duplicating an entity with a flow graph on it will also duplicate the flow graph, you can easily populate your level with entities that have custom game logic attached to them. This means that when an entity containing a flow graph is being copied, the flow graph it is attached to will also be part of the copied entity.

Overall, storing flow graphs this way gives you a lot of flexibility. To find the relevant flow graph data in your finished level, take a look at the corresponding .cry file. Once you save your level in CryENGINE Sandbox, the .cry file will be automatically created by the engine inside the level's folder. You can use a tool, such as WinRAR or 7Zip to open the .cry file and have a look inside.

If you take a closer look at the level.editor.xml file inside the .cry file, you will see that the flow graph structure is stored in a very similar way to the .xml file we exported earlier, as shown in the following code snippet:

```
<FlowGraph Description="" Group="Main" enabled="1"
  MultiPlayer="ClientServer">
  <Nodes>
    <Node Id="26" Class="Game:Start" pos="-200,720,0" flags="1">
      <Inputs InGame="1" InEditor="1"/>
    </Node>        </Nodes>
</FlowGraph>
```

So basically, the flow graph is just a property of the entity just like all its other properties.

The entity nodes with dynamic targets

Earlier in this chapter in the *Revisiting the basics of flow graphs* section, we discussed the different types of nodes and how both entity and component nodes can, or sometimes even require to, use entities.

An advanced technique often used in more complex flow graph setups is to dynamically input an EntityId into a node. This can be done in normal flow graphs, AIActions or flow graph modules. EntityId tells a flow graph node which entity to use and is used to identify any entity in the level.

[Each entity in the level has a unique entity identifier, EntityId.]

Before we start building more complex setups, however, let's start with the simple example of an entity node with a dynamic EntityId input:

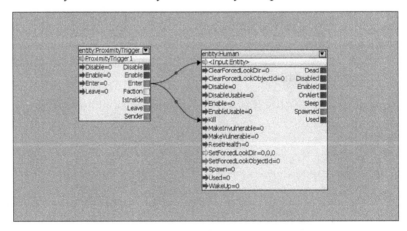

The flow graph setup kills the player once it enters the trigger

This simple flow graph setup consists of two entity nodes: A **ProximityTrigger** and a **Human** AI entity node. All this flow graph does is kill the AI unit that enters the trigger. This is very unfortunate for the poor AI unit entering the trigger, but very simple as far as the setup goes.

EntityId is provided by the output port of the **ProximityTrigger** node and is inserted into the EntityId port of the AI Grunt node. This will overwrite whatever EntityId was set for this node so far. Furthermore, the output is also connected to the kill input port of the **Human** entity. This leads to any **Human** AI entity that enters the trigger being killed instantly.

Earlier, we said that an entity node is always a representation of an entity existing on your level. This is true but it does not necessarily mean that the entity has to exist when the flow graph is being built.

In our preceding flow graph example, we use the EntityId node of the AI unit, which entered the proximity trigger. This AI unit might not have been placed manually by you and was maybe spawned sometime after the game started. Using a dynamic EntityId input, your flow graph will work with any entity, regardless of whether it was placed by you in the level or generated at run time. This gives you a lot of flexibility when setting up flow graphs.

What happens if we input the wrong EntityId?

You probably already noticed that when working this way, an invalid EntityId is provided to a node. Let's use our previous example to illustrate this. Maybe, for example, we forget to set up our **ProximityTrigger** properly and an entity was allowed to trigger the output port that was not of the type **Human** AI. In this case, our AI **Human** entity flow graph node will be provided with an EntityId of something else, such as a vehicle or a weapon, which does not have the same input ports defined.

If this happens, the engine might throw a warning into the engine console to notify you of what went wrong. How this is handled depends on the code of the node receiving the wrong input.

Although this will not crash your game, it most likely means that something is going wrong and should be fixed.

A more complex application of dynamic EntityIds

Let's extend our example a bit and evaluate the type of the entity that enters our trigger at runtime. Have a look at the following flow graph setup:

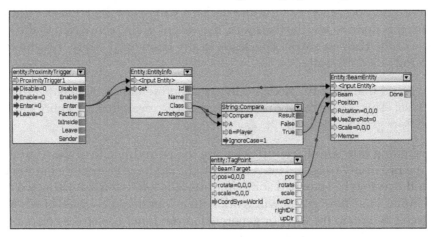

EntityId is used to determine the entity class

In the preceding flow graph setup, the **ProximityTrigger** node provides an **EntityId** node for the **EntityId** port of an **Entity:EntityInfo** node. The output is also used to trigger the **Entity:EntityInfo** node's **Get** input port, which outputs all relevant information of the target entity.

In our example, we use this information to look at the class of the provided entity and check if it equals **Player** using a **String:Compare** node. If this is true, EntityId is reused and fed to an **Entity:BeamEntity** node, which beams the entity to a predefined tag point location.

Basically, we built a simple teleporter logic that beams the player to a predefined position once the trigger is entered. This example can now be further extended by randomly selecting positions to beam the player. Add more criteria to check for the player or beam particle effects once the trigger is entered.

Let's take a shortcut

Before we look at some more advanced flow graph setups, let's look at the keyboard shortcuts for the flow graph. Like many other tools in Sandbox, the flow graph is rather complex and has a lot of features. Although most of those features can simply be accessed using the mouse, it is, of course, much more efficient to use keyboard shortcuts wherever they are available.

It is pretty much like playing a strategy game, for example, *StarCraft*. You can completely play it by just using your mouse, but you will be much faster when you take the time to learn the important shortcuts.

Let's look at the most useful flow graph shortcuts.

Q – node quick search

This one can almost be considered a hidden feature since it is so easy to miss. The node quick search shortcut (the Q key by default) is very useful when you are trying to find a node. Generally, there are two ways to add new component nodes to your flow graph. You can either use the **Add Node** functionality in the context menu or the component node list window to add new nodes.

The node quick search offers a convenient third way of adding nodes, that is, if you know what you are looking for. By pressing the Q key while you are working inside the flow graph window, the quick search menu will open and allow you to type in a node name. You don't even need to know the complete name of the node you are looking for since the quick search function will autocomplete it for you.

To make things even more comfortable, you can even use the arrow keys to cycle between the different nodes, which match the node name you entered.

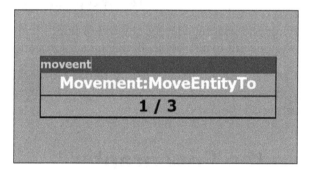

Node quick search allows you to quickly find nodes

F/G – link highlighting

With increasing complexity, your flow graphs can get harder to read. The more nodes and links you have in your flow graph, the harder it will become to follow the layout of the graph. This is where the link-highlighting feature will come in handy.

By pressing the F or G key while you have a flow graph node selected, you can highlight the incoming and outgoing links. This can help you to see which links are actually going into what ports.

Note that if you want to see just the links going out from or coming into a specific port, you can hover your mouse cursor over the port's icon. This will highlight all the links connected to the port in a different color.

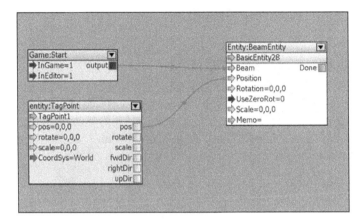

Ctrl + Shift + V – paste nodes with links

You are probably familiar with MS Windows and using the *Ctrl + C* and *Ctrl + V* shortcuts to copy and paste objects. To make things more comfortable, these have identical functions in the flow graph. You can easily copy and paste nodes this way.

However, when copying and pasting a larger amount of nodes that are connected with each other, it can be very useful to also paste all the links interconnecting the nodes.

By pressing *Shift + Ctrl + V* instead of just *Ctrl + V* to paste the nodes into a flow graph, all the links connecting the selected nodes will also be pasted. This saves you the work of reconnecting all the duplicated nodes.

Embedding the flow graphs

Flow graphs can become really powerful when being used as part of a prefab. Doing so is not really difficult since flow graphs are stored as a property of an entity. Embedding a flow graph inside a prefab, for example, is very simple. All you have to do is create a new prefab using an entity that contains a flow graph. The flow graph will automatically be saved within the prefab and will be available whenever the prefab is placed in a level.

Embedded flow graphs can be useful when the created prefabs are supposed to have a certain level of interactivity. Things such as the interior of a room—containing a TV, light switches, or other interactive objects—are quite easy to set up.

As an example, let us build a simple light switch that could be used inside a prefab. For this, we want to set up a **Light** entity that can be switched on/off using a **Switch** entity.

The following are the steps to build a light switch:

1. Create a simple setup containing a **Switch** entity and a **Light** entity.
2. Set up a simple flow graph that lets the **Switch** entity turn the **Light** entity on/off.
3. Create a prefab containing the **Light** and **Switch** entities.

The flow graph to operate the light entity can be built with a varying level of complexity. The example used here is rather straightforward and just uses two entities. The only thing to keep in mind when setting up this flow graph is that it should be created on one of the entities, which will be part of the prefab. Storing the flow graph on an entity not included in the flow graph will, of course, not save it when the prefab is saved. Our simple example flow graph is shown in the following screenshot:

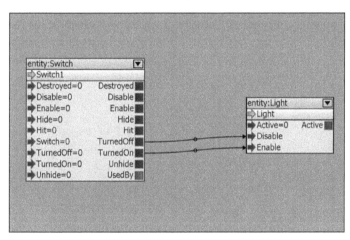

A simple light switch

In the preceding flow graph, the **TurnedOn** and **TurnedOff** output ports of the **Switch** entity are used to enable and disable the **Light** entity. By default, the **Switch** entity uses a placeholder 3D model. You can, of course, exchange it for a model that fits your project better. The type of model being used has no effect on the functionalities of the actual switch.

The next step after this is setup is to create a prefab that contains the flow graph logic we just built. This is very easy since all you need to do is select all the objects that are supposed to be part of your prefab—in this case, both the switch and the light—and select **Make From Selection** from the **Prefabs** menu:

Now that the prefab has been created, it is ready to be used and instances of it can be placed in a level. You may have already asked yourself how to actually access those flow graphs. They are embedded inside a prefab, so how can you get to them? If you look at your flow graph window, you will not see them as part of the entity graphs listed on the left-hand side of the window. It is designed this way to keep your flow graph window clean. You may potentially have dozens of prefabs in your level that have embedded flow graphs. If every single one would be visible all the time, your flow graph window would be pretty crowded.

Flow graphs embedded in prefabs can be accessed through the **Prefabs** section in the flow graph list window. However, only flow graphs in prefabs that are currently opened will be displayed. What that means is a prefab has to be placed and opened using the **Open** function in its **Properties** section in order for the flow graph to be visible.

 Only opened prefabs will be listed in the **Prefabs** section of the flow graph list window. Prefabs can be opened using the **Open** function in the entity's **Properties** window.

Once a prefab has been opened, you will see that the flow graph it contains will be visible in the **Flow Graph** list window:

The great thing about this simple setup is that it allows you to place the prefab anywhere and in any of your levels and have a working light switch without any extra work to set up the switch logic.

GameTokens

Flow graphs can be rather complex and include dozens of different nodes. Very often, it can be useful to work with variables to store and access gameplay information. This may include simple things such as counting a loop inside a flow graph or storing more complex information, for example, the number of times the player hit or missed the target.

This functionality is provided by the GameToken system. Game tokens can be accessed using flow-graph nodes, Lua scripts, or even C++. The most common way of working is through a set of provided flow graph nodes.

The following nodes provide you with access to the GameToken system:

- **Mission:GameToken**
- **Mission:GameTokenCheck**
- **Mission:GameTokenCheckMulti**
- **Mission:GameTokenGet**
- **Mission:GameTokenModify**
- **Mission:GameTokenSet**
- **Mission:GameTokenLevelToLevelRestore**
- **Mission:GameTokenLevelToLevelStore**

This set of nodes allows you to store all kind of gameplay information and use it to script complex game logic. A game token can store all kinds of information, including strings, numbers, and position information.

The GameToken libraries

Game tokens can be saved and stored either inside a CryENGINE level or in an external library that can be shared between levels. This provides a lot of flexibility, especially in projects with many different levels.

Whether you store your game token inside your level or in an external file has to be decided depending on what scope is desired for your game token variable. If the game token is most likely not used outside of one level, it does not make sense to store it in an external file.

Reaction to a game token changing its state

Besides the nodes, to get and set game tokens, there is also the **Mission:GameToken** node, which allows you to react to a game token changing its state. It is probably the most useful of all the game token nodes since it allows you to build complex game logic very easily.

A simple example of how to use it is shown in the following screenshot:

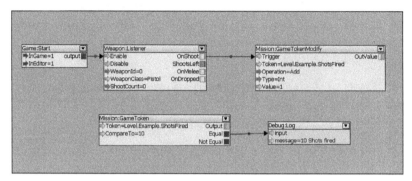

This flow graph shows the reaction to a pistol shot being fired

In the preceding screenshot, the game token system is used to count the shots fired from a certain weapon (in this case, a pistol) to trigger an output and log text into the console. A game token with the name **Level.Example.ShotsFired** has been created and a **Mission:GameToken** node is used to react to any change to the game token. The **Weapon:Listener** node triggers an output every time a shot from a pistol is fired. This triggers the **Mission:GameTokenModify** node and increases the value of the game token by **1**.

With this setup, the **Mission:GameToken** node is triggered every time the game token changes. It does not matter where the modification of the game token is done, the node will always trigger an output when the value of the game token changes. This means that game token nodes in different flow graphs or a call from C++ code will still trigger an output from the node.

However, it is important to remember that the node only reacts to a change in the value of the game token and not to the token being set in general. This means that if the new value that the game token is set to equals the value it currently has, the node will not trigger an output. Only a change of the game token's value will do this.

 Assigning a value to a game token does not generally trigger an output. Only changing the value of the game token will trigger an output of the **Mission:GameToken** node.

The GraphTokens variable

An alternative to using GameTokens are GraphTokens. Different from GameTokens, these variables are not accessible globally and can help prevent your GameToken libraries from growing disproportionately.

You may just want to store very basic and simple information inside a certain flow graph, for example, a counter for a loop or other information specific to the flow graph. In this case, using the GraphToken system might be the better choice. The GraphToken system can be considered the little brother of the GameToken system. It works almost identically and allows you to create and access game tokens. The difference between the two systems is that the GraphToken system stores its tokens locally inside the flow graph so that the tokens are used. Graph tokens cannot be accessed from outside of the flow graph they have been created in. The benefit here is that game token libraries are not being filled up with unimportant tokens only created to store information relevant to one specific flow graph.

GraphTokens can be created using the **Edit Graph Token** function in the **Tools** menu of the flow graph:

Graph tokens are accessed using the same set of nodes that are used when working with regular game tokens. Instead of selecting a game token inside one of the game token nodes, the name of a graph token can be provided as a string.

Accessing the Lua functionality

Sometimes, the ability to access a certain Lua function directly from the flow graph can come in handy. Instead of wrapping up a script call inside the script of another entity or another custom code to do it, Lua code can be executed directly from the flow graph.

The **Debug:ExecuteString** node allows you to input any Lua script directly into the node. Although this should not be used in actual production flow graphs, it can be very useful during development to quickly test and debug certain features.

Take a look at the following diagram:

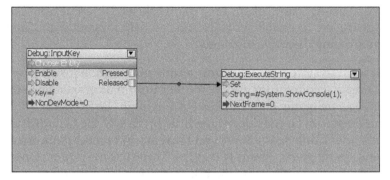

A Lua string executed using a flow graph node

In the preceding example, the **Debug:ExecuteString** node is used to show the in-game console when the *F* key is pressed. Keep in mind that calls to the Lua script need to be prefixed with a # symbol in order to be recognized as such.

Creating nodes in C++ and Lua

There are many different types of component flow graph nodes and even more entity nodes. Usually, all the existing nodes with their input and output ports provide enough functionalities even for complex scenarios and setups. However, new ports and nodes can be added easily, should you have the need for them. Let's start by adding a new port to an entity-based node.

Adding ports to an entity flow graph node

Almost every Lua script entity in CryENGINE has a FlowEvents table defined in its script. In this table, the input and output ports of the node and the corresponding functions are defined. The FlowEvents table of a **Light** entity, for example, looks like the following:

```
Light.FlowEvents =
{
  Inputs =
  {
    Active = { Light.Event_Active,"bool" },
    Enable = { Light.Event_Enable,"bool" },
    Disable = { Light.Event_Disable,"bool" },
  },
```

```
  Outputs =
  {
    Active = "bool",
  },
}
```

The `FlowEvents` table has subtables defining the inputs and outputs. Inputs are defined in the following format:

```
InputName = { EntityName.Event_FunctionName,"data type" },
```

The **Light** entity, for example, has the following line:

```
Active = { Light.Event_Active,"bool" },
```

This defines an input port called `Active` on the **Light** entity, which when triggered calls a Lua function called `Event_Active`. The `"bool"` parameter at the end of the lines defines the type of parameter, which is passed to the function. Following this structure, it is really easy to add new inputs to entity nodes.

Adding output ports works the same way. Just add another entry to the `Outputs` table, defining the name and type of the output. Those outputs can then be called using the following function:

```
BroadcastEvent(entity, sOutputName);
```

Here, `sOutputName` is the name of the output to call and `entity` is the identifier of the entity sending the event. When more specific output is needed, the following function can be used:

```
entity:ActivateOutput(sOutputName, param);
```

The `ActivateOutput` function triggers a specific output port with the parameter provided. Using those functions, an output port can be called from anywhere within the Lua script.

Creating flow graph nodes using the Lua script

Creating new flow graph nodes using only the Lua script is possible but not recommended. Although the functionalities for Lua-based flow graph nodes exist, it is not recommended to use them in a production environment. When completely new flow graph nodes are required, we recommend that you use C++ to create them. The Lua node creation is an unsupported feature that could lead to problems and errors when used. If you are still interested in how Lua-based flow graphs are created, you can have a look at the `Game/Libs/FlowNodes/` folder to see how Lua-based nodes are created and structured.

Creating flow graph nodes using C++

Creating a new flow graph node using C++ is quite simple and should always be your first choice when a new node is required. In particular, when the node implements a complex behavior and needs to perform at a high speed, C++ is the best choice. The official CryENGINE documentation provides great tutorials on how to create new nodes based on C++. Furthermore, the source code of many flow graph nodes is shipped with the CryENGINE FreeSDK and can be viewed and used as a reference.

Summary

In this chapter, we looked closely at the flow graph, CryENGINE's visual scripting system. You learned about using dynamic EntityIds to create complex flow graphs, flow graph shortcuts, and different ways to create new flow graph nodes. We also looked at how embedding flow graphs inside prefabs adds more flexibility to flow graph scripting.

With this deeper insight into the features and the functionalities of the flow graph, you will be able to script more complex game logic in a very short amount of time. In the next chapter, you will get an introduction into the facial animation system of CryENGINE and learn how to set up your character for lip synching.

4
Morphs and Bones – Creating a Facial Setup for Your Character

Having a beautifully modeled character with polished materials and shaders will certainly go a long way in capturing the players within your game and story. But animating the body will only get you halfway there. From a raised eyebrow to lips drawn up into a smile, nothing can convey emotions as directly as a facial expression. This chapter will teach you how to use the CryENGINE facial animation system and how to create a facial setup for your character. In this chapter, we will look at all the steps necessary to create the facial setup for your character, which includes the following points:

- Exporting the character's head
- Working with facial libraries
- Facial animation sequences
- Expressions and lip sync

After the setup is complete, the character will be ready for facial animation and lip synching, which will be covered in the second half of the chapter. The goal of this chapter is to provide you with all the techniques necessary to set up high quality facial animations.

Creating a facial setup for a character

Before a face can be animated using the CryENGINE toolset or loaded into the **Facial Editor**, your character needs a facial setup that the engine can load and understand.

This setup includes a properly exported head and facial library. This section will take you through both of these steps. 3ds Max will be used for exporting. Other software packages, such as Maya, will work in a similar fashion but will not be covered explicitly. Take a look at the following screenshot:

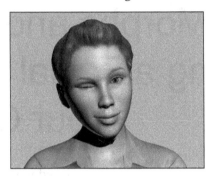

Note about morphs in CryENGINE

Up to and including Version 3.4.7, CryENGINE supports morphs as well as bone rigs for facial animation. With the release of Version 3.5, the support for morphs was officially dropped. This chapter will therefore use a bone rig for all examples and instructions.

It is possible that the support for morphs will be reinstated in a later release. In those cases where it makes a difference, an info box such as this will describe the workflow for morphs in addition to the bones.

Exporting the character's head

Any facial setup begins with the correct export of a head or a full body character. It is common practice to export the head separately from the rest of the body for multiple reasons. It allows the heads to be exchanged between different characters to create more variation. The other reason for this is that the head rigging or blend shape creation is often done by a different artist than the rest of the body (at least in larger teams that have multiple artists). Keeping the head in a separate MAX file allows an artist to work on the body and head at the same time.

You might regularly hear or read the term *blend shape* instead of *morph*. Different 3D applications, such as 3ds Max, Maya, and Blender use different names for the same concept. Both terms are interchangeable.

When creating a bone rig for the character's head, keep in mind that it has to be part of the main skeleton used for the rest of the body. Otherwise, you will not be able to attach your head as a **Skin Attachment** to your character in the engine.

Before you export your head, make sure your eye bones are named correctly. This is important for the LookIK feature to work inside CryENGINE. If you do not plan to use this, the bone names do not matter.

 If named correctly and LookIK is active, the bone rotations for the eye bones will be controlled by the engine. This can be counterproductive in some situations where you want to animate the eyes by hand. In this case, inserting a second pair of eye bones in the hierarchy right after the default ones can give that control back to you and keep the LookIK working.

Take a look at the following screenshot:

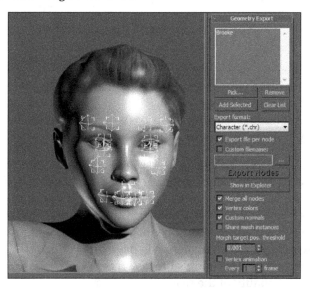

In the exporter settings for bones and morphs, you can export a bone rig as chr or skin

The morph workflow is shown in the preceding screenshot. When exporting morphs, create a `Morpher` modifier in the head mesh containing all the morphs. Make sure your head is in the **Editable Poly** mode. In the exporter settings, set the value for **Morph target pos. threshold** to `0.001` (or lower) and make sure that **Vertex animation** is unchecked. You are now good to export.

Using facial expression libraries

The facial expression library is the heart of all facial animation in CryENGINE. It maps morphs and bones to expressions.

Instead of working with morphs or bone animation directly, the CryENGINE facial animation system works with expressions. An expression is essentially a one-frame animation pose of the face. It can be put together out of multiple morphs and bone effectors, with different blend values. The expression for sad, for example, could consist of raised eyebrows, turned down lips, and a slightly dropped jaw.
The facial library contains a number of expressions, for example, for emotions and phonemes:

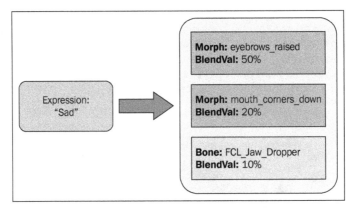

The facial expression library maps the expression names to the list of morph and bone effectors that the character was exported with. This library can be created manually or semiautomatically using the provided tools and the Facial Editor. Internally, CryENGINE works only with the expressions.

The reason behind using expressions instead of the bones and morphs directly is simple. It is completely independent of character and facial setup. Different characters might have different facial setups. For example, while the important characters of the game might have a high quality morph setup, the background characters might merely have a simple bone rig with a small number of joints. In a case like that, the story characters and the background characters will have different facial libraries, but map the same expression names. This allows the designers to play the same expressions on all faces. The visual quality of the result depends on the character's facial setup.

This is especially important for lip synchronization of audio. The names of the expressions for the different phonemes are fixed, but depending on the character's facial setup and expression library, they can be mapped to as many or as few morph or bone effectors as desired.

Morphs

Depending on your production pipeline and experience you might already have a preference for either bones or blendshapes. You do not have to choose one over the other. CryENGINE characters can have a mixed setup of bones and morphs.

Creating a new facial expression library

When you are creating a new character with a facial setup, you will need to create a facial expression library for it as well. The exception to this rule is when you already have a library for a different character with exactly the same facial setup, that is, the same facial bone rig and/or the same blendshapes. In that case, you can share the same library and will not need to repeat the setup.

Facial expression libraries have the file extension FXL and are stored in the XML format. You can open the library with a text editor, but it is not advisable to edit them like this. There are two ways to create a new library — manually in the **Facial Editor**, or semiautomatically through 3ds Max.

Manually creating a library

The fastest way to create a new facial expression library is to open the **Facial Editor** in Sandbox and go to **Expression Library | New**. Since you only want to create a blank dummy file at this point, you don't need to load a character first. You will be asked to provide a location to save the FXL file. Common places to save shared facial libraries are in a shared subfolder inside either the `Animation` or the `Objects/characters` folder. If your character has his/her own unique library, you might want to save it in the same folder as the exported head mesh. This makes it easier to move the character to a different folder later, or remove it clean from your game if you no longer need it.

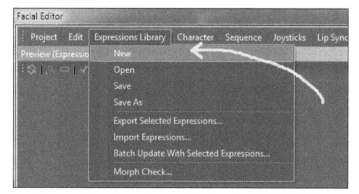

Expression libraries can be created easily using the Facial Editor

This will create a completely blank facial expression library. You will have to add in all expressions manually and assign blendshapes or bone effectors. This might be desired in some cases, but as the automatic generation from 3ds Max prefills the library with the most common expressions, such as the list of visimes and phonemes, it is generally recommended to use that as a starting point instead, to save time and effort.

Automatic creation

The **Facial Expressions Tool** included in the CryMaxTools of CryENGINE consists of a tool to create facial libraries semiautomatically. The scripts are mainly intended for a bone-based facial setup and can take animation keys from the timeline to put them into the library as expressions.

The most powerful feature of the entries for all visimes and phonemes that CryENGINE and the standard lip sync software packages are using. It will create time tags for it in the 3ds Max timeline. This way you can animate your face according to the time tags, export the library, and have a character ready for lip sync in no time.

Even if you don't plan on using lip sync at the moment, this library is a good place to start. It will save you the time of having to manually add in all phonemes later in case you need them.

> The CryMaxTools come with the CryENGINE SDK, but must be manually installed. They are located in the `Tools/CryMaxTools` folder. Execute the `copyToMax.bat` file to install both the tools and the exporter, automatically.

Bone rig requirements

The facial bone rig needs to meet a few requirements to work properly with the scripts of the Facial Expressions Tool, in regards to naming, hierarchy, and alignment:

- You will need to make sure that all your facial bones are world aligned and start with the prefix, `FCL_`. This prefix will allow the scripts to recognize which bones to include in the export. Instead of bones you can also use dummy objects.

- Make sure all bones that are needed to create your facial expressions are included. The exception to this naming convention is the eye bones. Those should be named `eye_right_bone` and `eye_left_bone`.

- The facial bones also need to be in a completely flat hierarchy, that is, one facial root bone directly parenting all facial bones. Otherwise, the scripts will export the facial expressions incorrectly. Of course, almost all facial rigs include a more complex hierarchy. It is therefore recommended to create a second bone rig for exporting purposes that fulfills these hierarchy requirements and link/constrain it to your actual control rig. Rename the root bone of your original control rig so that it starts with an underscore to prevent it from being exported.

 When exporting skeletons, the exporter will stop following down the hierarchy as soon as it finds a bone with a name that starts with an underscore (for example, `_Posing_Helper`). You can use this to prevent bones from being exported into the engine.

Creating expressions in 3ds Max

Now it is time to create the facial expressions that will later be exported to the engine. For a bone-based facial setup, the **Facial Expressions Tool** can be quite powerful, because it allows you to set up the different facial expressions in Max and export them directly into CryENGINE. Take a look at the following screenshot:

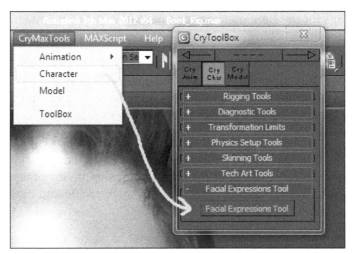

The Facial Expressions Tool can be found inside the CryMaxTools menu

To open the **Facial Expressions Tool**, open the **CryToolBox** for characters via the **Character** menu inside the **CryMaxTools** option. Make sure you have your skinned head mesh selected before opening the tool, as it will automatically try to work on the current selection. Take a look at the following screenshot:

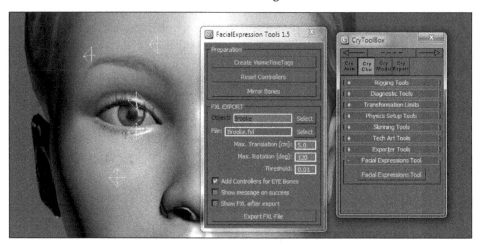

The Facial Expression Tool allows detailed control of the facial expressions

Before anything else, use the button labeled **Create VisimeTimeTags**. This will create 13 time tags for the timeline; one for a neutral expression, one for blinking, and 11 visimes for lip synching.

You can now animate your facial bones to match the time tags to create the various facial expressions. The scripts will use the 11 visimes on export and automatically assign them to the 40 different phonemes. This is the fastest way to get your character prepared for lip syncing. Make sure that your character's face is in a neutral pose in the first frame.

Each frame on the timeline can be exported as an individual expression to the facial expression library. You can add your own expressions to the list of visimes and you will most likely want to do this. This allows you to create and manage your expression library almost entirely in Max.

When adding your own expressions, you will need to create a new time tag for it on the timeline. The name of the tag must start with the prefix Exp_ so that the script can recognize this as a facial expression to be exported. Keep in mind that only the animation of the bones starting with the FCL_ prefix is exported, so do not include other bones in your expressions. Those will be missing in your facial library.

When you are done creating your facial expressions, use the button **Export FXL-File** to create your facial expressions library. It will be created in the same place as the Max file.

Creating a Facial Library with Morphs

When using morphs instead of a bone rig, you can still use the **Facial Expressions Tool** to create an FXL file. There will be entries for all phonemes even though they will be empty. This will give a good base to start from, and you can then simply assign morphs to those expressions. This is faster than creating blank expressions for all 40 phonemes manually.

Morph Workflow

When you load a head mesh with morphs into the **Facial Editor** for the first time, the tool will automatically extend its facial library with the morphs found on the head. You can then save the library again and start assigning the morphs to expressions.

Mapping the library

Before you can use your facial expression library and your exported head in the **Facial Editor** in Sandbox, you will need to map the library for the head mesh. This mapping is done in a `chrparams` file.

If you try to open your head mesh without a `chrparams` file containing a mapped facial library in the current CryENGINE release, you will receive an error message about a CAL file. The message text in this warning is outdated, as CAL files were the predecessors of `chrparams`. Don't let this irritate you—you are simply missing an entry in your head's `chrparams` file.

Your head mesh will need its own `chrparams` file, which will tell the engine the facial library to load and where it is located. Simply create a new text file in the same folder as your head's exported `chr` file and change the extension to `chrparams`. The file can be edited with any text editor, like Notepad. The file must have the same name as the head, just a different extension. So if your head is called `female_head.chr`, then the file you need to create needs to be called `female_head.chrparams`.

The content of the file is very less. The following code snippet is a sample that loads a facial library with the name `Brooke.fxl`. You can use this for your own character. Simply change the name of the file in the `path` attribute to your own.

```
<Params>
  <AnimationList>
    <Animation name="$facelib" path="Brooke.fxl" />
  </AnimationList>
</Params>
```

Not every character needs their own facial library. If you have the same facial setup for multiple characters, meaning the same bone rig and/or the same morphs, you can create and maintain just one library and share it among those characters. You will still need to create a `chrparams` file for all your individual head meshes, but they will reference the same FXL file for the facial library.

Creating expressions

After mapping the FXL file in the `chrparams` file, you can open your head in the **Facial Editor**. The **Facial Editor** in Sandbox can be accessed by navigating to **View | Open View Pane | Facial Editor**. You can either open the `chr` file directly, or open the `cdf` file of your entire character. In case you exported your head as a skin file, you will have to create a `cdf` file first, using the **Character Editor**, as the **Facial Editor** cannot open skin files directly.

Once you load a character navigating to **Character | Load**, the facial library will be automatically loaded as well. You can see the available effectors, morphs, and expressions that your character has available. Now you can either create new expressions or modify existing ones.

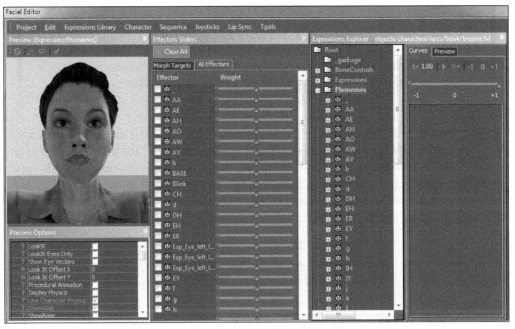

The Expression Explorer is very useful when browsing expressions

All expressions are listed on the right-hand side, in the **Expression Explorer** pane. The expressions contain one or more bone effectors or morphs, and blendvalues. When you select any of the expressions in the **Expression Explorer** pane, you can preview the blended result on the character's face in the preview window.

You can also create entirely new expressions here. Apart from lip sync visimes, phonemes, and blinking, you might want to have additional expressions, for example, for moods, such as happy, angry, or sad.

Facial Mocap software (Brekel Kinect Face, Faceshift, Live Driver, and so on) also often requires that a character has certain expressions available. If you want to work with those, you will need to create the correct expressions in the **Facial Editor**.

To create a new expression, right-click on the **Expression Explorer** pane and choose **New Expression**. Then choose a name for your new expression. It should not contain any whitespaces. You can also move your new expression into a subfolder. Those folders are just there to keep the large amount of expressions organized visually; they serve no further purpose. Take a look at the following screenshot:

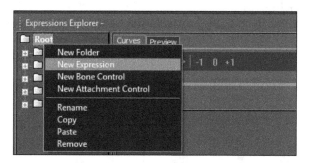

New expressions can be created directly in the facial editor

You can create new expressions directly in the **Facial Editor** by blending together the ones you already have. The workflow for bones and morphs is a little different.

For bones, you can drag-and-drop effectors from the **Effector Sliders** window onto your expression to add them to it. Then you can adjust the weight of each effector you added. Usually, you don't want each effector to be blended in 100 percent. You might, for example, just want to raise the eyebrows a little bit instead of all the way for an expression called suspicious.

To adjust the weight with which the individual effectors should be blended together, select the expression and right-click on the **Curves** window. From the pop-up menu, choose **Change Weight**. The weight should be between zero and one. By default, the value will be set to **1**.

In the same way that you can adjust the weight of effectors in existing expressions, you can add/remove effectors from them as shown in the following screenshot:

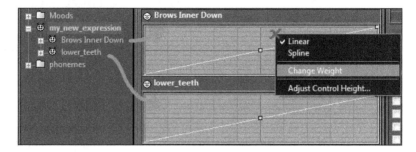

The weight of an effector can be tweaked for each expression

The same workflow can be applied to morphs, but when using morphs exclusively there is a more convenient way to create the expressions.

You can use the sliders in the **Morph Targets** tab to create the facial expression that you like directly in the preview window. When you are happy with the result, choose your new expression in the **Expressions Explorer** pane, right-click on it and choose **Initialize From Sliders**. This will only work for morphs; other effectors will have to be added via drag-and-drop as described earlier in this section:

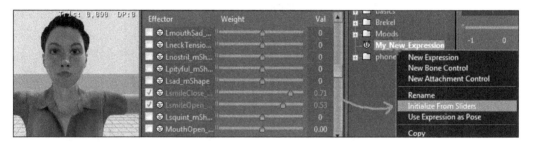

Slider settings can be used to create expressions

Facial animation

Once you have a facial library full of expressions to work with, you can start creating facial animations with the **Facial Editor**. A facial animation file is called a facial sequence and is saved as an FSQ file. These can be played back on a character using **TrackView** or **FlowGraph**. As facial sequences only reference expression names, they are character independent.

When using a bone rig, you can of course animate the bones directly in 3ds Max or Maya and export it as a partial body animation using the CryENGINE exporter. For some Mocap pipelines or phoneme extraction tools, this might be a preferable pipeline.

Creating facial sequences

Now, it's time to start creating the actual facial sequences. To create a new facial sequence, perform the following steps:

1. Open the **Facial Editor** and select the **New** option in the **Sequence** menu.

2. A file dialog window will open where you can give your new sequence a name and choose a location in which to save it.

3. Like other animations, facial sequences should be stored inside a subfolder of the `Animations` folder. You can pick the location you prefer, but you have to save the sequence within a subfolder of CryENGINE, otherwise it won't work.

4. Next, you will have to set the duration for your new sequence. To do so, click on the **Properties** button of the sequence to open the **Facial Sequence Timing** dialog, and adjust the **End Time**.

 The duration is specified in frames not seconds. A value of 30 will create a sequence that is 1 second long. You can modify this duration later. If you have a sound loaded, you can even adjust the length of the sequence to automatically match the sound.

The time of a facial sequence can be changed to fit exactly

You can now start adding expressions to your sequence. To do so, drag-and-drop expressions from the **Expressions Explorer** pane into the **Root** folder of the sequence (to the left-hand side of the timeline).

You can then adjust the blend value of each expression on the timeline. The animation curves use the same controls as the **TrackView** editor. Double-click on the spline to add a key, and double-click on a key to remove it. You can adjust the tangents using the tangent toolbar above the timeline.

You can preview your animation anytime by hitting the play button, or manually scrub through the timeline. Once you are done, make sure to save your sequence again, using the **Save** option in the **Sequence** menu:

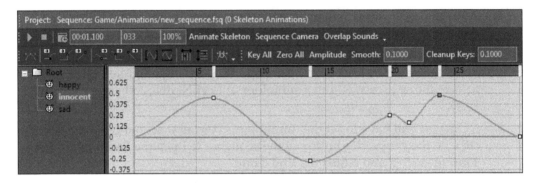

Splines can be edited to create smooth blend values

Using facial sequences in the engine

After you have created one or more FSQ files for your character, you can play them back using **TrackView** or **FlowGraph**. But before the engine allows you to play them, they will need to be added to the character's animation list. Just like animations, facial sequences will only be available for a character if they have been mapped through a `chrparams` file.

As this book tries to focus on advanced topics, we assume that the reader is already familiar with mapping animations inside the character's animation list. Please also take a look at *Chapter 7, Animating Characters*, for further tips on mapping animations.

Lip sync sequences are the exception to this rule, as they do not need to be mapped. See the *The Lip Sync feature* section inside this chapter for more information.

Inside the TrackView editor

The **TrackView** editor in Sandbox is used to set up in-game cut scenes. Adding a facial sequence to a cut scene is a great way to deliver information even without dialog lines. Facial animation can be used to express moods and reactions of a character and make them appear more alive.

After adding your character entity to the **TrackView** sequence, you will need to add an additional track for facial animation. Right-click on your entity in the sequence, choose **Add Track**, and select **Facial Sequence**.

Double-click on the timeline to add a key to this track. In the **Key Properties** window, open the **Facial Sequence** drop-down box to see a list of all mapped facial sequences that have been loaded for this character. After one is chosen, the key on the timeline will adjust itself to represent the correct time for the facial animation:

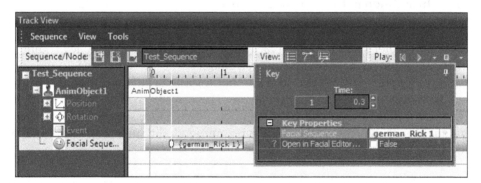

Facial sequences can be played using the facial editor

 When previewing facial animations in the **TrackView** sequences, make sure you also have a full body animation playing on that character. Otherwise, the head of the character will start spinning slowly around its own axis.

Inside the FlowGraph node

The FlowGraph node used to play facial sequence files on a character is called **Actor:FacialAnim**. This node offers a little more control over the sequence playback than the **TrackView** node, as it is meant to be used during interactive gameplay and not during a premade cut scene. Take a look at the following screenshot:

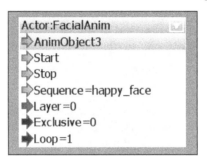

The facial animation node

Different from the **TrackView** editor, the sequence name must be typed in manually, as there is no drop-down box allowing the user to choose from the list of loaded sequences. In addition to the sequence name, there are extra parameters that can be specified.

The **Layer** parameter specifies which facial animation layer the sequence should be played on. Multiple sequences can run on a character at the same time, for example, one for the mood, one for lip sync, and another for idle behavior. These layers are different from the full body animation layers. There are seven layers available, so valid values for this parameter are the numbers 0 to 6. Since some layers are used by systems such as lip syncing or the AI, it is recommended to use either layer 0 or 6 for the **FlowGraph** node.

The parameter **Exclusive** will suspend playback on all other facial animation layers. This can be useful if the node is used to trigger a one-time facial reaction on the character, for example, a smirk, a wink, or a painful expression.

The **Loop** parameter determines whether the sequence will be played just a single time, or should repeat indefinitely until stopped. Idle behaviors, which could include eye jittering and blinking and a general mood might need to be played in a loop, while other sequences are designed as single-shots.

 Even though the **FlowGraph** node for playing facial sequences is in the category **Actor**, all entities can use this node. It will work just as well with **AnimObjects** or GeomEntities, as long as they have a character loaded.

Using expressions

A facial animation sequence is usually an animation consisting of multiple expressions and it is several seconds long. Expressions are blended in and out over the course of the duration of the animation. But sometimes a whole sequence is not needed to add a little more life to your character. You can also use expressions from the facial expression library directly.

Using a simple expression instead of an authored sequence is a quick way to add some attitude to your characters. You can, for example, add a mood expression onto your character, such as raised eyebrows, a smile, squinting eyes, or an expression of fear. Take a look at the following screenshot:

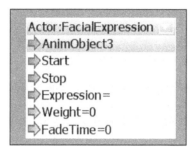

The FacialExpression node can play a facial expression directly

The **FlowGraph** node used to start and stop expressions on a character is called **Actor:FacialExpression**. Since expressions are essentially one-frame animations, all expressions are played on loop, indefinitely. They can be stopped using the same node.

Like with the node for facial sequences, the name of the expression must be typed in manually. Any effector from the facial expression library can be chosen. Use the **Weight** parameter to adjust how far the expression should be blended in, for example, how much the eyebrows should be raised, or how broad a grin should be. Values should be in the range of zero to one.

The **FadeTime** parameter is the equivalent of the **blend time** parameter for full body animations and controls how fast the expression should be blended in. The time is specified in seconds and will be used for both the blend in and the blend out.

 The **TrackView** editor also offers a track for facial expressions. However, this track type only supports morph targets. Since the current version of CryENGINE does not support morphs, this track is presently obsolete.

The Lip Sync feature

During cut scenes or regular gameplay, if your characters are supposed to talk, you will want them to move their mouth while they do so. Ideally, the lip movements match the audio from the voice line exactly. This is called lip syncing.

Manual lip synching

There are multiple approaches to accomplish lip syncing, depending on the level of detail you are aiming for. A very simple solution, for example, is to create just one single facial sequence that moves your character's jaw and lips a little for a few seconds to make it look like it is talking. And then you trigger this animation on a loop every time your character speaks.

Alternatively, you can manually create a facial sequence for each of your wave files in the **Facial Editor**. The next few lines show you the workflow for this approach.

First load a wave file into a sequence by navigating to **Sequence | Load Sound**. Then add phonemes by right-clicking on the **Lip Sync** track at the bottom of the timeline and choose **Insert** to select from a list of phonemes. By using the slider to scrub through the timeline, you can hear the sound file and see how well your lip sync matches the audio. Take a look at the following diagram:

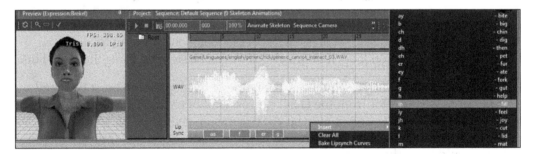

Automatic phoneme extraction

More advanced solutions use software tools to analyze the recorded voice line wave file to create a list of phonemes that can then be played back through the facial animation system. For this to work, your character needs to have a facial expressions library that contains these phonemes. If you created the library through the included CryMaxTools, your library will already have these entries.

There are several commercial tools available to extract phonemes from wave files and there are even some available for free. Each tool will output the extracted information in a different format, ranging from FBX animation files to simple text files. The choice of which tool to use is largely dependent on your personal preferences, experiences, and budget.

Open source phoneme extraction tools might generate an output of a lower quality, but some of them are available as open source (AnnoSoft offers a free version of their software including source code, for example). This means their code can be modified to output CryENGINE-ready FSQ files.

The advantage of automatic extraction is that it requires very little manual work. In a good pipeline, the phoneme tool is run over all recorded voice lines and the lip sync FSQ files are automatically created. Within minutes, all dialogs in a game can be lip synced, even for multiple languages.

If you have a facial motion capture pipeline working, another option to gather the lip sync animation is to record it directly from a human speaker or actor. The animation can even come from a different actor than the original speaker (as long as it matches the audio). On the upside, this approach can record emotions along with the lip movement, saving time in the post processing. On the downside, every single file of every language needs to be recorded manually this way.

Lip sync playback

The lip sync information for a voice line is stored inside an FSQ file, just like regular facial animations. Different from those, however, the created files do not need to be mapped inside a `chrparams` file to be loaded. The facial animation system will automatically load them dynamically when asked to lip sync with a sound.

When playing back an audio file using **TrackView** or **FlowGraph**, an additional parameter tells the engine whether this sound is a voice line and it should be lip synced. If this parameter is set, then the engine will automatically try to find and play the correct FSQ file. The flag that needs to be set for this automatic behavior is called voice and it works with both the dialog through FMOD as well as playing the sound files directly. The FSQ file must have the same filename as the audio file (except for the extension) and be placed in the same folder.

If the lip sync sequences were created with an automatic tool, they will likely already be in the right place and named correctly, so there is no more work to be done. If the lip sync was created manually, you will need to make sure to put the files in the folders with the wave files.

When you are playing sounds using the **Sound:PlaySound** FlowGraph node, the flag can be set by setting **Voice** to true:

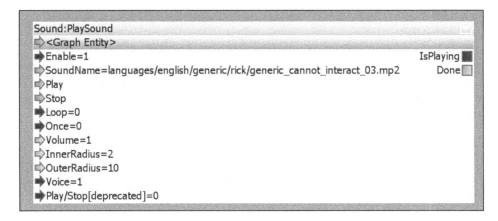

In **TrackView**, the key properties of a sound key in the **Sound** track have checkboxes for **Voice** and **Lip Sync**. Both need to be checked for the automatic playback to work:

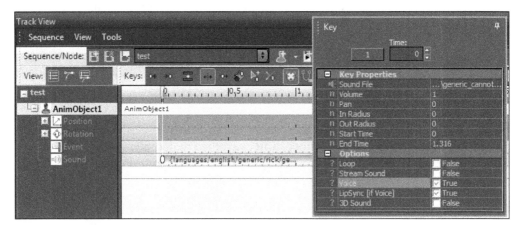

When starting a sound with the code, using the **SoundProxy:PlaySoundEx** function, you will need to provide the flag **FLAG_SOUND_VOICE** as a parameter.

The automatic playback is meant for lip sync data that was extracted or created offline. There are libraries available that can extract lip sync information live on the fly. If you want to work with them, you can do so by simply triggering the phoneme facial expressions from the expression library directly at runtime.

Quality

There are two major aspects that define the visual quality of the lip sync: the quality of phoneme extraction and the quality of the facial expressions. Also, adding emotions on top of the lip sync can be the icing on the cake.

Quality – phoneme extraction

When lip synching is done manually, the output depends entirely on the skill of the user. The various automatic phoneme extraction tools differ in the quality of the results they produce. The free tools, especially, sometimes struggle to create good extraction with languages other than English.

A manual polishing pass is recommended to go over those automatically created files and fix errors. However, using automated tools can quickly produce a base for lip synching, as all dialog in the game can be processed in one go. Then the polishing can be done as a second pass, as time permits. This approach allows prioritizing work, where the lip sync for dialogs in important story cut scenes can receive more attention and polishing than in-game voice lines, where the automated lip sync might be sufficient.

Quality – visimes and phonemes

Even the best phoneme extraction is useless if the face doing the lip sync doesn't have a lot of variation in its expressions. The more capable your facial rig or your morphs are, the better your face will look when animated.

The **Facial Tool** in the CryMaxTools will only ask you to create 11 visimes for the character's face. The script will then use these to create the required 40 different phonemes from them. This is a very fast way to get a character ready for lip synching, but you will achieve a better quality when modeling each of the phonemes individually. You can of course use the visimes to start out with and then replace the phonemes later in the production, when and if you have the time and resources to do so.

A typical game project includes characters of different quality levels. The main hero and important story characters (often called A-level characters) are usually of a higher quality and apart from having more polygons and higher texture resolutions, they will likely have a more complex facial setup as well. Background and side characters (C-level characters) will probably have simpler setups consisting of just a few bones or morphs. Since the lip sync facial sequences are character independent, you can use the same lip sync sequences for all of these characters, though the results will look different on each.

Quality – adding emotions

Phoneme extraction, manual or automatic, will only provide you with information on how to move a character's lips and mouth. But to truly make your characters come alive, you will need to throw some emotions in the mix. A voice line said in anger will look more believable if the speaker narrowed his eyebrows and flared his nostrils while speaking. With the exception of using facial motion capture, the only way to achieve this is to add additional expressions to the lip sync sequences manually.

Another approach is not to add the mood and emotions into the lip sync sequences directly, but to play them back separately and along with the voice lines. Remember that you can play more than one facial sequence on a character simultaneously. That is what the facial animation layers are meant for.

You can trigger an angry expression or even a facial sequence along with the sound file using **TrackView** or **FlowGraph**. The advantage of working that way is that you won't have to manually modify the lip sync files for every language you wish to support. Since dialog lines sometimes change and need to be recorded again, this approach can also save you time by not having to redo this step every time a sound file is exchanged.

Summary

This chapter gave you an introduction into the CryENGINE facial animation system. It explained facial expression libraries and the different approaches to lip synching. You have learned how to create facial animations and how to play them in the engine using **FlowGraph** and **TrackView**.

With the instructions in this chapter, you will be able to create a facial setup for your own character and prepare it for lip synching.

The next chapter will reveal some hidden secrets of the CryENGINE Sandox editor, a feature that you likely didn't know existed, and shortcuts that can save you time during production.

5
Mastering Sandbox

After having mastered the facial animation pipeline of CryENGINE, it is now time to look at one of the most important tools in the CryENGINE SDK package: Sandbox. **CryENGINE Sandbox** is more than just a level editor used to place objects. It combines many tools with very different functionalities and is a lot harder to learn and master than your average 3D level editor.

Getting the most out of Sandbox requires you to know all its ins and outs, its hidden features, and little quirks. In this chapter, we will take a look at all the little secrets Sandbox tries to hide from you.

Don't stop getting better

Before we go ahead and start looking at specific features or shortcuts, it is important to talk a bit about the way we usually work with software such as CryENGINE.

When you start learning something new, like a 3D engine you have never used before, your skill level will increase rapidly at the beginning. The first time you used Sandbox, for example, you were probably struggling to build even a simple level and remember where the most important features were located.

After using Sandbox for a few weeks or months, however, all those basic tasks such as exporting a level or generating a terrain texture became second nature and you probably didn't have to think about them much anymore.

At this point, when you have reached a skill level high enough to get the job done, you will usually stop improving and learning new skills. This happens with most things you learn in life. Once you get to a skill level where you are 'good enough' to get the job done, you will stop improving.

This is what journalist and author Joshua Foer calls the "OK Plateau". It describes the habit of subconsciously saying "I am good enough at this". In his book, *Moonwalking with Einstein*, Foer describes the OK Plateau as follows:

> *"…that point when we reach the autonomous stage and consciously or unconsciously say to ourselves, "I am OK at how good I have gotten at this task," and stop paying attention to our improvement. We all reach OK Plateaus in almost everything we do. We learn to drive when we're teenagers, and at first we improve rapidly, but eventually we are no longer a threat to old ladies crossing the street, and we stop getting appreciably better."*

> — *Joshua Foer, Moonwalking with Einstein*

This is important to keep in mind when working with a technology such as CryENGINE. Make sure you always remind yourself to not stop improving, even if you always get your tasks done in time and are happy with what you deliver.

There is always another shortcut to learn that will speed up your work, and always another macro you can create to automate time intensive steps in your workflow.

Keep this in mind as we look at all the different features and shortcuts in this chapter; they will help you get better, faster, and more comfortable with CryENGINE Sandbox.

Getting faster with keyboard shortcuts

Let's start with the easiest way to speed up your workflow: keyboard shortcuts. Using keyboard shortcuts in Sandbox is just the same as using them in any of your favorite games. Have you ever played a strategy game or an MMO without using shortcuts altogether? It is certainly possible to just use the mouse and none of the many shortcuts available when you guide your character through the depth of a virtual dungeon, but would you do it? Probably not, since using shortcuts is much less exhausting and you can use them without looking at the screen and constantly travelling with your mouse to the various buttons on the user interface.

This is the same for using Sandbox. There are plenty of shortcuts for all kinds of features, and by making use of those, you will not only increase the speed at which you work, but also work in a more relaxed manner because you reduce the amount of mouse movement needed.

Thinking about hand placement

The design and layout of Sandbox has been inspired by various tools and games. While the general layout of the user interface might remind you of 3D Studio Max, the basic controls of Sandbox have been designed with gaming controls in mind. It starts with things like the camera control in Sandbox. The combination of mouse movements combined with classic *WASD* keyboard controls resembles first-person shooter controls very closely. Looking at the Sandbox keyboard layout, you will notice that most of the functionality is concentrated on the left side of the keyboard.

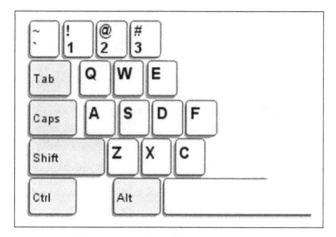

Most commonly used Sandbox shortcuts

This is where all the shortcuts for camera movement, object editing, and selection are located. Looking at this layout, it becomes clear why it makes most sense to put your left hand on the left side of the keyboard with the middle finger resting on the *W* key, similar to the position used when playing a first-person shooter game.

From this position, all of Sandbox's important functions can be reached without moving your hand over the keyboard.

Handedness: Sandbox's default shortcut layout was not designed with left-handed users in mind. However, this is not a big problem, since Sandbox allows you to customize and remap all shortcuts to more convenient locations on the keyboard. Have a look at **The Toolbar Menu** section in the CryENGINE documentation for more information on customizing shortcuts at `http://docs.cryengine.com/display/SDKDOC2/The+ToolBar+Menu`.

Object editing modes

Let's start with the most important keyboard shortcuts. Your most commonly used shortcuts next to the WASD camera controls should be the *1, 2,* and *3* keys. Those keys let you quickly switch between the three main object editing modes, which are as follows:

- Movement (*1*)
- Rotation (*2*)
- Scale (*3*)

Of course, Sandbox's user interface offers you buttons to switch between those modes.

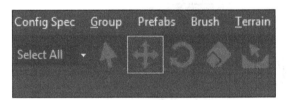

User interface elements for object editing modes

You should, however, not use those buttons to switch between editing modes ever. Instead, only use the shortcut keys.

One of the most important ways to increase your production speed is to minimize the way your mouse has to travel. Every time you click on one of those buttons to change between the editing modes, your mouse has to travel all the way up to where the button is located and then back to where the object you are currently editing is.

The difference between using the *1, 2,* and *3* keys to switch between the editing modes and click on the respective buttons is huge.

Test it!

Try it out yourself. Open a level in Sandbox and try building a simple village composed of a couple of houses which are arranged alongside a curved road. You can use the assets provided in the SDK or your own game's assets for this.

Try not using any shortcuts at all and measure the time it takes you to build a simple village setup. Then redo the same task, forcing yourself to only use shortcuts, and never click on the buttons.

When you compare the time you take for the two tasks, you will notice how much faster you were when you were only using shortcuts.

Not only will you be faster, but also your eyes do not have to travel all the way up to the button along with your mouse when you switch modes. This helps your brain to stay focused on what you actually want to achieve.

 Object editing mode: Never use the user interface buttons to switch between the movement, rotation, and transformation modes. Force yourself to use the *1*, *2*, and *3* key shortcuts instead to gain a significant increase in production speed.

Aligning objects

Although not really a hidden feature and even briefly mentioned in the official CryENGINE documentation, the object alignment shortcuts are easily overlooked.

There are two very convenient shortcuts which will allow you to place an object exactly where you want it with a single mouse click, without unnecessary adjustment of position and rotation. Those shortcuts are *Shift* + *Ctrl* + left-click and *Shift* + *Ctrl* + *Alt* + left-click.

With an object selected and in the object movement mode, simply keep the *Shift* and *Ctrl* keys pressed and left-click anywhere in the perspective view to place your object. This looks like a rather simple feature, but it is extremely useful when aligning objects with each other or the terrain.

Let's say you have to stack a couple of crates on top of each other in your level. Doing it manually would require you to first align a crate on the *x* and *y* axes of another crate and then adjust the *z* axis value until it fits exactly. This is time consuming and certainly not a fun task to do. By using the object alignment shortcuts, however, you can easily stack ten or more crates on top of each other in a matter of seconds.

The extended version of this shortcut (*Shift* + *Ctrl* + *Alt*) is even more useful in complex setups, since it will also align the object to the surface normal of the target object or the terrain position clicked. Placing a rock object naturally onto the side of a mountain becomes very easy when the extended alignment shortcuts are used.

The pivot position of the currently selected object will be used to align it to the normal of the surface clicked. This works for terrain as well as for complex assets with a high polygon count.

Multiple objects easily aligned by using the alignment shortcuts.

Being able to quickly align objects with each other will save you a lot of time in everyday-productive situations.

 Object alignment: The object alignment shortcuts *Shift + Ctrl +* left-click and *Shift + Ctrl + Alt +* left-click make it easy to align objects to each other or with the terrain.

Using the deep selection feature

The deep selection feature is relatively new in CryENGINE and has only been added to the engine with Version 3.1.0. These shortcuts allow you to accurately pick one specific object, even if it is overlaid by several others in the perspective view. The deep selection shortcuts are as follows:

- *Tab* + left-click
- *Tab* + Z + left-click

The levels you create for your game might get filled up with objects quickly. Having an object count of several thousand is not uncommon for a normal CryENGINE level. Selecting objects in those environments can be quite difficult, especially if objects are overlapping each other. This can be caused by physics proxies overlapping or objects just being placed very close together.

When trying to select an object which is overlapped by another object, the deep selection feature lets you cycle through all the objects which are under your mouse click.

To use the deep selection feature, simply keep the *Tab* key pressed when selecting an object. Each mouse click will now cycle through all objects under your mouse cursor. Every time you perform a left-click, the next object in line will be selected for you.

The feature even offers you a simple-to-use drop-down list when you press *Tab* + *Z* instead of just using the *Tab* key.

The key combination *Tab* + *Z* has been chosen rather unfortunately, since *Z* is also the default key for the **Goto Selection** function, which allows you to jump directly to an object's position.

You might want to remap this shortcut to another key to avoid confusion when using the deep selection feature.

Drop-down list showing objects in deep selection range

Deep selection range: Keep in mind that only objects within the deep selection range will be taken into account for this feature.

The deep selection range can be changed in the Sandbox preference settings by navigating to **Preferences | General Settings | General | Deep Selection | Range**.

Using the Goto Selection feature

The ability to directly jump to a selected object is very useful and should be used extensively. By using the **Goto Selection** feature, you can jump to any selected object directly. This feature becomes even more useful when the respective shortcut is utilized to activate it. By default, the **Goto Selection** feature is mapped to the *Z* key.

In combination with the Sandbox object finder window, this shortcut allows you to rapidly jump around your level and select different objects without even moving the camera once.

Objects accidently placed below the terrain surface or outside of the level border can be found quickly by using the **Goto Selection** feature.

Using camera tag-points

In addition to the ability to move the camera to specific objects, it can be extremely useful to have Sandbox memorize arbitrary camera positions.

Your everyday work on a level might involve working on multiple different locations within the same .cry file. This might include work on locations for cutscenes, actual gameplay locations, or maybe specific camera positions used during performance profiling tasks.

Instead of constantly moving the camera between different work locations within the level, you can just create so-called camera tag-points and use them to quickly jump between different, far away locations within your level.

The shortcuts to do this are as follows:

- *Ctrl + F1* to *F9*
- *Shift + F1* to *F9*

To set a new camera tag-point, simply move the camera to a desired location and press *Ctrl + F1* to *F9*. For example, *Ctrl + F1* would set the camera's tag-point number 1 to the current position of your camera.

Once a camera tag-point is set, CryENGINE will provide you with a short confirmation in the Sandbox console window of the newly created tag-point. You will see a log entry that looks similar to this:

```
Camera Tag Point 1 set to the position: x=187.80, y=127.07, z=24.58
```

In addition to this log entry in the console, CryENGINE will also write the position into a file called `tags.txt`. This file is located within your level folder and stores all camera positions which have been set.

To import/export saved camera positions, you can simply copy the file between the different level folders.

To recall a stored camera position, simply press *Shift + F1* to *F9*. For example, *Shift + F1* would jump to the camera position which has been previously stored with *Ctrl + F1*.

Top five shortcuts

Before we finish talking about shortcuts and move on to the various customization options Sandbox has to offer, let's compile a list of the top five CryENGINE Sandbox shortcuts. You might already know some of them while you might have never used others.

What all these shortcuts have in common, however, is that when you start making them a part of your everyday workflow, you will gain a great increase in production speed.

Here we go! The following are the top five shortcuts every CryENGINE developer should know and use:

- *Shift + Space*: This turns object helpers on and off. It is much faster than using the user interface buttons.
- The Space bar: Hold the Space bar pressed when object helpers are turned on to see all entity selection helpers for all entities. This comes in very handy when selecting objects hidden behind other geometry.
- *Ctrl + T*: This brings up the object finder window.
- *F* and *Ctrl + F*: The *F* key freezes the selected object and puts it on the freeze list. The *Ctrl + F* combination unfreezes all frozen objects in the level.
- *H* and *Ctrl + H*: The *H* key hides the selected object and puts it on the hidden list. The *Ctrl + H* combination unhides all hidden objects in the level.

Of course, these are not all the useful shortcuts Sandbox has to offer, but these five will probably be among your most commonly used ones.

The more you force yourself to use shortcuts instead of relying on the user interface, the greater the effect on your production speed will be.

Customizing Sandbox

The default window layout of Sandbox was designed to best utilize the available screen space and is usually a good choice for most standard situations.

However, don't forget that you can customize Sandbox completely to your needs and make it fit for the tasks you are currently working on. Depending on what you work on, the default Sandbox setup might not be your best choice.

For example, a window setup that is good for editing in-game cut scenes might not be optimal for AI setup tasks or working on confined interior locations.

For everyday work, it can make sense to create various Sandbox layouts and then switch between them depending on the task you are currently working on.

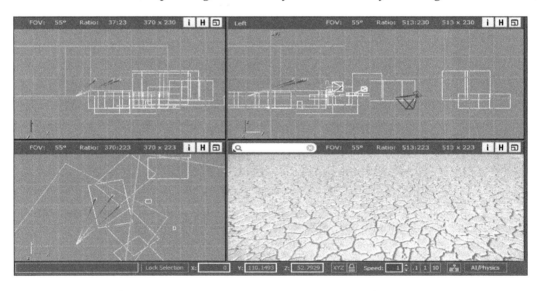

Sandbox UI split up into four different viewports

Customizing the Sandbox window layout

CryENGINE offers you a lot of possibilities when it comes to defining your main viewport. While for most basic level design tasks one big perspective viewport might be a good choice, sometimes more overviews can be useful.

The **Configure Layout** option lets you pick how you want to split your main viewport. Especially when working on smaller locations with objects aligned on a grid, it can be useful to have the ability to quickly switch between the **Top**, **Front**, and **Perspective** views.

If you prefer to work with only one viewport, most likely the **Perspective** view, remember that you can quickly switch between all available views using *Ctrl + Tab*.

This way, you can switch between views quickly without compromising on screen space.

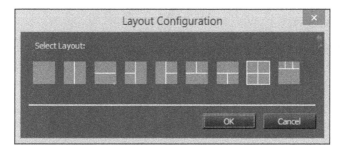

Sandbox lets you select your preferred window layout

Saving and loading layouts

The ability to load and save Sandbox window layouts is very comfortable and can be utilized to build and store layouts for almost any situation.

Try to have the best possible layout stored for the most common standard situations such as AI setup, cut scene editing, and performance profiling. You can also share those saved layouts among your team. It might, for example, be useful for a new team member to see what the recommended window layout for a standard situation looks like.

Working with cameras

Camera entities are quite useful. They are mostly utilized in TrackView sequences, but can also be used for pre-caching locations or making screenshots. Placing cameras is simple, since a camera entity can just be dropped into the level from the **RollUpBar**.

Camera targets

A nice and very well hidden feature is the ability to manipulate the camera target independently from the camera itself. Usually, when placing a camera entity, Sandbox will not create a camera target entity for you to work with. If you would like to have access to the camera target, you have to create the camera entity the following way:

1. Left-click on the camera entity in the **Object/Misc** section of the **RollUpBar**.

2. Move the mouse over your level terrain and click and hold the left mouse button.

3. Move the mouse and release the left mouse button to place the camera target in the level.

Quite well hidden, isn't it? However, once you know the trick, it becomes easy to create cameras with a separate camera target. The target acts as an independent entity, which can be used in flow graph or TrackView.

Building a cut scene with the camera rotating around a character or following an object this way is very easy. You can just manually link the camera target to any entity you like and the camera will always follow it.

You could even dynamically link the camera target in flow graph, triggered by a TrackView event, to have the camera look at different objects dynamically.

The camera target is a normal entity with its own entityID and can be used in flow graph or script for all kinds of things, just like a regular entity.

A camera with a camera target entity, created by holding the left mouse button while placing a camera

Camera target: By default, cameras are created without a camera target. Press and hold the left mouse button when creating a new camera to create a separate camera target entity to work with.

Switching cameras

There are many ways to switch between the cameras placed in your level. The viewport options allow you to switch to a different camera and you can also use the context menu of a selected camera to make it the active camera.

However, you probably didn't know about the camera switching shortcut, since it is quite well hidden and almost undocumented.

Simply press *Ctrl + ~* to cycle between all cameras placed in the level. This is a very useful shortcut and will save you the time of always opening the viewport options menu to switch to a different camera.

 Switching cameras: *Ctrl + ~* is an undocumented shortcut and will let you switch quickly between different cameras.

Exploring Sandbox custom commands and macros

CryENGINE has hundreds of different console variables which let you customize every aspect of the engine. Things such as rendering, audio, or the user interface can be customized and debugged on the fly using a plethora of console variables.

The console allows you to quickly type in any console variable to turn on a certain debug mode or check a specific setting. You can access the console both in the Sandbox editor and in game.

When you are debugging a certain issue or continually testing a behavior in the same way, it can make sense to set up a macro for those console variables you use over and over again. Using a macro is a lot faster than always typing your command in the console, especially when this macro is then bound to a shortcut.

Sandbox offers a nice and easy-to-use macro editor, which lets you bind all kinds of commands and scripts to a button or key.

The macro editor can be found in the **Tools** menu under **Configure ToolBox Macros**.

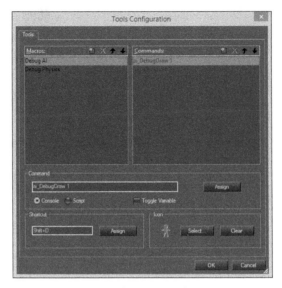

The Sandbox macro editor

This is where new macros can be created and bound to a shortcut. A macro can consist of one or more console variables or even a custom Lua script to be executed.

When debugging an AI problem, for example, it would make sense to create a macro that switches on all relevant AI debug modes using multiple console variables. Then, instead of setting all of them manually, a single key-press can switch an extensive set of debug variables on and off.

Or you could reload a certain set of entity scripts on the fly by just pressing one button to call a macro, which is bound to a script that reloads several other scripts automatically.

This extensive kind of debugging and testing work is where the macro system will come in handy. And in case you don't want to put every macro on its own shortcut, you can simply access the macro list from the **Tools** menu under **ToolBox Macros** and drag the macro list out as a separate window. This way, you can have your most important macro buttons floating in a window somewhere easy to click when you need them.

Sandbox custom commands and macros

Sandbox macros are stored in a simple XML format, which allows you to easily export them to another machine. You can find your macros in the ../USER/ folder. The file Macros.xml contains all your defined macros.

You could even edit your macros directly in the XML file if you need to do some quick adjustments.

Looking at some lesser-known features

CryENGINE Sandbox is more than just a simple level editor. Countless small tools with different functionalities are hidden in this huge, powerful editing tool. In this section, we will shed some light on a few not-so-well-known features which are part of Sandbox.

Video recording

CryENGINE offers many ways to record videos out of the engine. You can use a TrackView sequence, which is rendered into a video or a simple console command. This starts rendering out single frames at a fixed frame rate.

But did you know that Sandbox features a simple-to-use AVI recorder, which lets you record videos directly out of Sandbox, including sound? The built-in AVI recorder can be found in the **Display** menu under **AVI Recorder** and lets you record videos directly from Sandbox.

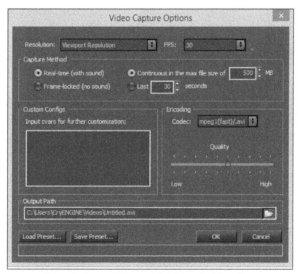

A ready-to-go AVI recorder is part of Sandbox

Capturing videos this way might not provide you with the highest quality video output, especially if you compare the results to single frames rendered out individually. However, the ease of use of this feature makes it a very convenient solution if you need to create some quick video captures of your project.

Mesh editing

Although the best way to create assets for CryENGINE is to build them in a **DCC** tool such as 3ds Max and then export them into the engine, Sandbox offers the tools to edit 3D models directly.

Did you know you can make changes to an object's mesh directly in Sandbox?

Only **Brush** objects can be edited in Sandbox. Complex entity types such as Lua-based entities cannot be edited and have to be converted into a Brush first.

The **Sub Object Mode** function in the **Edit** menu lets you edit the mesh of a Brush directly and work with the vertices, edges, and faces of the 3D model.

Of course, the mesh editing functionality in Sandbox is quite limited, especially if compared to a professional **DCC** tool. However, small changes and edits can be made easily. Furthermore, the edited mesh can then be saved as a new object using the **Save CGF** functionality of the selected Brush.

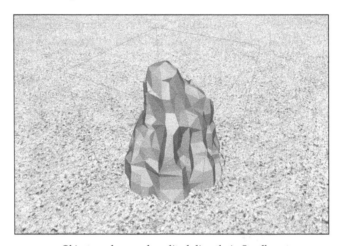

Object meshes can be edited directly in Sandbox

Physics proxies: Keep in mind that editing an object's mesh in Sandbox does not make any changes to the physics proxy of the object. Physics proxies cannot be edited in Sandbox and all changes have to be done in a **DCC** tool.

Managing PAK files

Did you know you can create and edit CryENGINE .PAK files directly in Sandbox? The **PAK Manager** option in the **File** menu lets you create, delete, and edit engine PAK files for your game.

A .PAK file can contain all kinds of files needed for your game, your mod, or even a single level you have built. Instead of shipping a bunch of files to your users, you can just use the PAK Manager to wrap everything up properly in one file which is easy to ship.

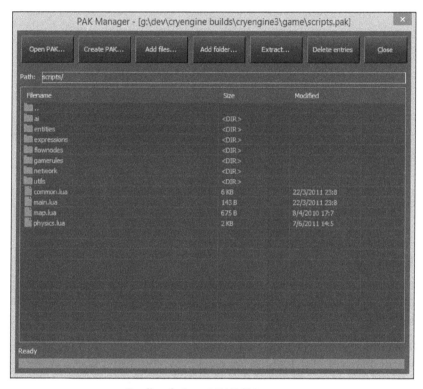

Sandbox features a PAK file manager

Keep in mind that the number of files and folder structures inside a .PAK file can be defined in any way you want. You can include level files, audio files, textures, assets, and anything else you might need for your game inside one .PAK file.

Renaming multiple objects

You probably knew that you can rename any object in Sandbox by editing its name property in the **RollUpBar**.

Very often overlooked, however, is the **Rename Object(s)** feature, found in the **Modify** menu, which lets you rename multiple objects at once. What is so special about this feature?

Imagine you have a hundred objects placed in your level, all with different names. In order to rename all those objects to something like `Environment_Object_` followed by a number, you would have to rename all the objects individually. The **Rename Object(s)** function allows you to select multiple objects and then set one name for them. For example, if you select a hundred objects and enter the name `Environment_Object_`, all the objects will be renamed `Environment_Object_1` to `Environment_Object_100`.

The Rename Object(s) interface

This simple feature will save you a lot of time when cleaning up levels and sorting through objects.

Summary

In this chapter, we looked at a lot of small but important features of Sandbox, all of which should help you become faster and more confident when working with the Sandbox editor.

The Sandbox editor is a huge tool, and even after working with it for many months, you might still discover new features or workflow you didn't know about.

In the next chapter, we will take a closer look at the Lua script implementation of CryENGINE and learn how to utilize Lua scripts to quickly and efficiently prototype and build gameplay without the need to recompile C++ code.

6
Utilizing Lua Script in CryENGINE

Gameplay in CryENGINE can be created in many different ways. The engine offers you full C++ code access as well as an easy-to-use visual scripting system called flow graph. Both approaches have upsides and downsides; it depends on what type of work you would like to do.

While access to the C++ source code gives you full power to change anything in the engine, it requires more time to make changes since the code always has to be compiled before it is run. Furthermore, a certain level of knowledge is needed in order to write and compile the C++ code properly.

The flow graph, on the other hand, is very easy to use and makes it easy for you to visually script gameplay and test it right away. Even without any coding knowledge, you can build a complex setup within a few minutes by using the flow graph. The downside of the flow graph, however, is that a complex setup can become very tedious to create and there are limits to the complexity a flow graph can have.

This is why CryENGINE has a Lua script implementation that bridges the gap between these two powerful systems.

In this chapter, we will look at some of the most important topics that we encounter when working with the Lua script in CryENGINE:

- Creating new Lua script entities
- Making entities multiplayer-ready
- Working with the state machine
- Using the script binds

Understanding the relevance of the Lua script in CryENGINE

The Lua script is used extensively in CryENGINE. Many entities, such as AI behaviors or game rules, are created by using the Lua script. The accessibility and the ability to reload any script at runtime makes Lua a nice middle ground between the complexity of C++ and the ease of use of the flow graph. The role of a developer in the production environment determines how much Lua will be used on a day-to-day basis to perform certain tasks.

Although easy to learn and very flexible, the Lua script has its pitfalls. For example, as the language is strongly typed, this makes things a bit more difficult since mistakes can easily go unnoticed for a while.

A level designer, for example, does not usually touch C++ code, but might now and then create a new entity type by using Lua. A C++ developer, on the other hand, will do most of their work directly in C++ and only sometimes work with Lua to create new script binds or AI behaviors.

While simple tasks will most likely always be done using the flow graph, more complex and performance-intensive tasks should be done in C++. Take a look at the following diagram:

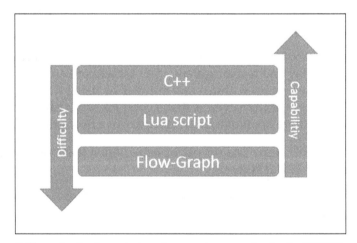

Different levels of complexity when creating gameplay for CryENGINE

Lua-based entities

Most entities you can place in CryENGINE Sandbox are based on the Lua script. This means these entities have a script proxy attached to them. This script proxy provides you access to a Lua table that contains the entity information and various functions. These Lua tables let you add new properties or functions to an entity.

Creating a new Lua script entity is easy and can be done within a few minutes without recompiling any code.

Creating a new Lua-based entity

Only a few steps are necessary to create a new Lua script entity. Firstly, an entity definition file, a so-called .ent file, has to be created. This file registers the Lua entity with the engine and points to a script that will be used. The entity definition files are placed in the ../Game/Entities/.. folder.

Let's create a new entity by first creating an .ent file with the name Testy.ent and place it in the ../Game/Entities/.. folder. For our example, we will just call our entity Testy, but you can change the entity name to something different. Just make sure you change both the name of the .ent file and the corresponding .lua file.

The content of your .ent file should look as follows:

```
<Entity
  Name="Testy"
  Script="Scripts/Entities/Others/Testy.lua"
  />
```

This will register a new entity called Testy with the engine and use the Lua script ../Game/Scripts/Entities/Others/Testy.lua for it.

Optionally, you could add the Invisible="1" property to the .ent file to prevent the new entity from showing up in the Sandbox entity selection. This might be useful if you would like to disable your entity temporarily instead of deleting the actual entity files. This can also be used to make entities available to the engine but prevent the user from placing them manually.

Before this can work and your entity can be used in Sandbox, however, we need to first create the actual Lua script and place it in the correct directory.

In order to do this, simply create a new text file called Testy.lua in the ../Game/Scripts/Entities/Others/.. folder.

The content of your new Lua file should look like the following:

```
Testy = {
  Properties={

  },
  Editor={
    Icon="User.bmp",
  },
}
```

Please note that for this example, we put the `.lua` script for the entity inside a folder called `Others`. You could, of course, put the script into any other folder inside your `Scripts` folder by changing the folder name to something different.

This is all we need to create a new entity using Lua. Once you start Sandbox, you will be able to place your new entity from the `Entity/Others` folder in **RollupBar**. Of course, there is not much going on right now with our entity since we have not added any functionality to it yet.

We created a basic entity table with two subtables; one is called `Properties` and the other is called `Editor`. While the `Properties` table will later hold all our entities' properties, the `Editor` table contains information about how entities will be displayed in Sandbox.

```
Icon="User.bmp",
```

The previous line of code, for example, defines the helper icon that is displayed in Sandbox to identify our entity. These icons are located in the `../Editor/ObjectIcons/..` folder. You can change the icon used or add your own icons by copying the respective bitmap files to this folder.

Although our entity is technically working, we will now extend the script a bit to allow us to use some functionality later. Each Lua-based entity should at least have the following tables and functions:

- A `Properties` table that defines the entity's properties
- An `Editor` table that defines the editor properties of the entity
- An `OnInit()` function that is called at game start
- An `OnReset()` function that is called when the entity script is being reloaded
- An `OnPropertyChange()` function that is called whenever a property has been changed

Let's add these to our script and restart Sandbox to make the changes take effect. Please note that restarting Sandbox is not always necessary in order to make the changes effective in our script. Only for changes at a low level, such as adding an OnReset() function, does Sandbox need to be restarted. In most cases, the **ReloadScript** button in **RollupBar** will do the job.

Reloading scripts

For most changes, it is sufficient to use the **Reload Script** button found below the entity properties in **RollupBar**. Sometimes, however, when the script changes are made at a low level, Sandbox needs to be restarted for the changes to take effect. This is the case, for example, for changes to scripts such as Player.lua and BasicActor.lua.

The entity script of our little Testy entity should look like the following:

```
Testy = {
  Properties={
  },
  Editor={
    Icon="User.bmp",
  },
}

functionTesty:OnInit()
  self:OnReset();
end;

functionTesty:OnReset()
end;

functionTesty:OnPropertyChange()
  self:OnReset();
end;
```

This is pretty much all that the script needs to have a working Lua entity. From here on, all kinds of properties and functions can be added. A new property can simply be added in the property table as shown in the following code snippet:

```
bTest = 1,
```

This will make your entity table look like the following:

```
Testy = {
  Properties={
    bTest = 1,
```

```
      },
      Editor={
        Icon="User.bmp",
      },
    }
```

After reloading the entity script, you will see a new property checkbox called **Test** in **RollupBar**. The variable prefix b is used to tell Sandbox to present the property in the form of a checkbox. You can use various prefixes to let Sandbox know what type of information the property is supposed to store. This makes it easier for the user to set up certain entity properties. You can chose between the following variable prefixes:

- b for Boolean
- f for float
- i for integer
- s for string
- clr for color
- object for an object compatible with CryENGINE, such as a CFG, CGA, CHR, or CDF file

These prefixes make it a lot easier to set up entity properties. For example, if the object prefix is used, Sandbox will display a small folder icon next to the property value. You can then click on that icon and a file open dialog will be displayed which lets you select a CryENGINE-compatible 3D model. This is way more comfortable than typing in the filename yourself.

Assigning a 3D object to an entity

An entity in CryENGINE can have one or more 3D models assigned to it. However, this is not a prerequisite for a functioning entity. Not all entities need to have a 3D model attached to it. In some 3D engines, a 3D model is placed in the scene and then a script or behavior is attached to it. In CryENGINE, it works the other way around. A 3D model is assigned to an entity or used by an entity script. The entity, however, is rather independent from the 3D model and might even change it at runtime if required. To illustrate this, let's load a 3D model for our new entity.

You have probably noticed that when you place our new Testy entity in your level, you will not see much. If you turn on the display helpers in Sandbox, you will see the small gizmo that lets you grab and move the entity and the icon that we assigned in the Editor table within our script, but that is about it. To load a 3D model for our entity, we need to specify a file and load it into a slot of our entity.

Using entity slots

Each entity provides so-called entity slots that can be used to load different things. You could, for example, load a 3D model and a light or particle effect into an entity slot. Once an object has been loaded into a slot, you can decide whether a specific slot should be visible or not.

This architecture allows you to load multiple objects and effects into an entity and switch between them easily during runtime. The simplest way of using an entity slot is to load a 3D model into it and set it to visible.

Let's modify the OnReset() function of our entity. A typical call would look like the following code snippet:

```
functionTesty:OnReset()
  local props=self.Properties;
  if(not EmptyString(props.fileModel))then
    self:LoadObject(0,props.fileModel);
  end;
  self:DrawSlot(0,1);
end;
```

This function will load the object specified in the fileModel property of the entity into slot 0 of the entity. Please note that we have not added the fileModel property to our property table yet. We will do this in the next step.

Let's have a look at the individual lines of the OnReset function:

```
local props=self.Properties;
```

The first line just declares a new local variable called props, which we will use to access the entity's properties. The next line is given as follows:

```
if(not EmptyString(props.fileModel))then
  self:LoadObject(0,props.fileModel);
end;
```

This block first checks if the provided string for the filename is not filled by using the EmptyString helper function. Then, the LoadObject function is used to load the file defined in the fileModel property into entity slot 0 by using the following line of code:

```
self:DrawSlot(0,1);
```

This last line finally sets the slot 0 as visible. At this point, we could go on and load more objects into other slots and then draw them, but we will keep things simple in this example.

As a last step, we need to add the actual `fileModel` property to the entity:

```
Properties={
  fileModel = "",
},
```

With this property added, you can easily select a 3D model in Sandbox. After performing the last step, the property table should look like the following screenshot:

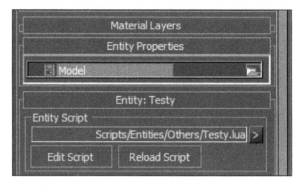

The entity property window with a new property

Remember that after every change you make to your script, you can simply use the **ReloadScript** button in the **RollupBar** to reload your script. No need to restart the engine every time you make changes!

After you have added this property, changed your `OnReset function`, and picked a 3D model for your entity, you should see it being rendered in Sandbox.

If you are unsure which 3D model to use, just go with anything in the `/objects/default/..` folder, for example, `../objects/default/primitive_box.cgf`.

Now we have a working entity that we can use for all kinds of things, and we can extend it with more script functionality:

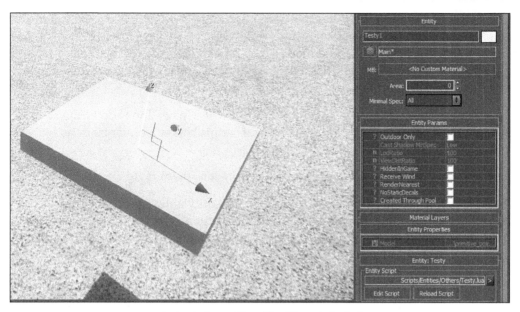

A simple Lua entity with a 3D mode loaded

Setting up physics

You might have noticed that the new entity does not yet behave physically correct. It has no collision and does not collide properly with other objects in the level. This is because we have not set up the physical properties for the object yet. Luckily, doing this is quite easy and can be achieved by adding only a few lines of script.

Firstly, we have to add the `Physics` properties table to our entity. With the physical properties added, our property table should look as shown in the following code snippet:

```
Properties={
  fileModel = "",
  Physics = {
    bRigidBody=1,
    bRigidBodyActive = 1,
    Density = -1,
    Mass = -1,
  },
  },
```

The `Physics` table we added to our `Properties` table is pretty basic and provides values for the entities' mass, density, and rigid body behavior. There are many more values which can be added and edited to tweak how an entity reacts physically with the environment. For most entities, however, the basic values for mass, density, and rigid body should be enough.

Once the `Physics` table has been added to the script, we need to modify the `OnReset()` function to do the proper physical setup. This can easily be done by adding the following line to the function:

```
EntityCommon.PhysicalizeRigid(self,0,props.Physics,0);
```

This function will apply the `Physics` table to the entity and register the entity with the physics system. The `PhysicalizeRigid()` function is one of the many helper functions found in the `EntityUtils` script that can be found in the `..\Scripts\Utils\..` folder.

> The `..\Scripts\Utils\..` folder contains a number of scripts that contain many helper functions. These are very useful when working with the Lua scripts in CryENGINE. Make sure you browse through the scripts to see what functions are available for you there.

After adding the code to physicalize the entity, our `OnReset()` function should look as shown in the following code snippet:

```
function Testy:OnReset()
  local props=self.Properties;
  if(not EmptyString(props.fileModel))then
    self:LoadObject(0,props.fileModel);
  end;
  self:DrawSlot(0, 1);
  EntityCommon.PhysicalizeRigid(self,0,props.Physics,0);
end;
```

With these changes made, the entity should now behave physically correct. The values for mass or density, for example, can now be changed directly in Sandbox without the need to change the script any further.

Making an entity multiplayer-ready

In order to make our entity work properly in a multiplayer environment, certain changes need to be made to our script.

Right now, we are not taking into account whether our entity is operating on a client or a server. Let's go ahead and get our entity network ready. For this, we need to make sure the server serializes the script entities properly.

Understanding the dataflow of Lua entities in a multiplayer environment

When using your own Lua entities in a multiplayer environment, you need to make sure everything your entity does on one of the clients is also triggered on all other clients. Let's take a light switch as an example. If one of the players turned on the light switch, the switch should also be flipped on all other clients.

Each client connected to the game has an instance of that light switch in their level. The CryENGINE network implementation already handles all the work involved in linking these individual instances together using network entity IDs. Each light switch can contact its own instances on all connected clients and call its functions over the network. All you need to do is use the functionality that is already there.

One way of implementing the light switch functionality is to turn on the switch in the entity as soon as the OnUsed() event is triggered and then send a message to all other clients in the network to also turn on their lights. This might work for something as simple as a switch, but can soon get messy when the entity becomes more complex. Ping times and message orders can lead to inconsistencies if two players try to flip the light switch at the same time.

The representation of the process would look like the following diagram:

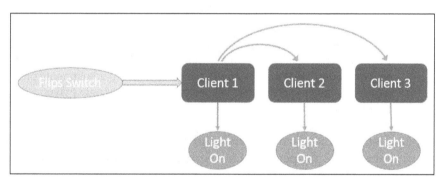

Not so good – the light switch entity could trigger its own switch on all network instances of itself

Doing it this way, with the clients notifying each other, can cause many problems. In a more stable solution, these kinds of events are usually run through the server. The server entity—let's call it the master entity—determines the state of the entities across the network at all times and distributes the entities throughout the network.

This could be visualized as shown in the following diagram:

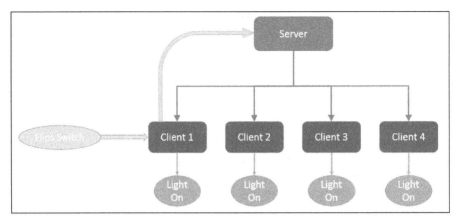

Better – the light switch entity calls the server that will distribute the event to all clients

In the light switch scenario mentioned earlier, the light switch entity would send an event to the server light switch entity first. Then, the server entity would call each light switch entity, including the original sender, to turn on their lights.

It is important to understand that the entity that received the event originally does nothing else but inform the server about the event. The actual light is not turned on until the server calls back to all entities with the request to do so.

> The aforementioned dataflow works in single player as well, as CryENGINE will just pretend that the local machine is both the client and the server. This way, you will not have to make adjustments or add extra code to your entity to check whether it is single player or multiplayer.

In a multiplayer environment with a server and multiple clients, it is important to set the script up so that it acts properly and the correct functions are called on either the client or the server.

The first step to achieve this is to add a client and server table to the entity script using the following code:

```
Client = {},

Server = {},
```

With this addition, our script table looks like the following code snippet:

```
Testy = {
  Properties={
```

```
        fileModel = "",
          Physics = {
            bRigidBody=1,
            = 1,
            Density = -1,
            Mass = -1,
          },

     Client = {},
     Server = {},

     Editor={
       Icon="User.bmp",
     },
   }
```

Now, we can go ahead and modify the functions so that they work properly in multiplayer. We do this by adding the `Client` and `Server` subtables to our script. This way, the network system will be able to identify the `Client`/`Server` functions on the entity.

The Client/Server functions

The `Client`/`Server` functions are defined within your entity script by using the respective subtables that we previously defined in the entity table. Let's update our script and add a simple function that outputs a debug text into the console on each client.

In order for everything to work properly, we first need to update our `OnInit()` function and make sure it gets called on the server properly. Simply add a server subtable to the function so that it looks like the following code snippet:

```
functionTesty.Server:OnInit()
  self:OnReset();
end;
```

This way, our `OnReset()` function will still be called properly. Now, we can add a new function that outputs a debug text for us. Let's keep it simple and just make it output a console log using the CryENGINE `Log` function, as shown in the following code snippet:

```
functionTesty.Client:PrintLogOutput(text)
  Log(text);
end;
```

This function will simply print some text into the CryENGINE console. Of course, you can add more sophisticated code at this point to be executed on the client. Please also note the Client subtable in the function definition that tells the engine that this is a client function.

In the next step, we have to add a way to trigger this function so that we can test the behavior properly. There are many ways of doing this, but to keep things simple, we will simply use the OnHit() callback function that will be automatically triggered when the entity is hit by something; for example, a bullet. This way, we can test our script easily by just shooting at our entity.

The OnHit() callback function is quite simple. All it needs to do in our case is to call our PrintLogOutput function, or rather request the server to call it. For this purpose, we add another function to be called on the server that calls our PrintLogOutput() function.

Again, please note that we are using the Client subtable of the entity to catch the hit that happens on the client. Our two new functions should look as shown in the following code snippet:

```
functionTesty.Client:OnHit(user)
  self.server:SvRequestLogOutput("My Text!");
end

functionTesty.Server:SvRequestLogOutput(text)
  self.allClients:PrintLogOutput(text);
end
```

We now have two new functions: one is a client function calling a server function and the other one is a server function calling the actual function on all the clients.

The Remote Method Invocation definitions

As a last step, before we are finished, we need to expose our entity and its functions to the network. We can do this by adding a table within the root of our entity script that defines the necessary **Remote Method Invocation (RMI)**. The Net.Expose table will expose our entity and its functions to the network so that they can be called remotely, as shown in the following code snippet:

```
Net.Expose {
  Class = Testy,
  ClientMethods = {
    PrintLogOutput = { RELIABLE_UNORDERED, POST_ATTACH, STRING },
  },
```

```
    ServerMethods = {
      SvRequestLogOutput = { RELIABLE_UNORDERED, POST_ATTACH,
        STRING},
    },
    ServerProperties = {
    },
  };
```

Each RMI is defined by providing a function name, a set of RMI flags, and additional parameters. The first RMI flag is an order flag and defines the order of the network packets. You can choose between the following options:

- UNRELIABLE_ORDERED

- RELIABLE_ORDERED

- RELIABLE_UNORDERED

These flags tell the engine whether the order of the packets is important or not. The attachment flag will define at what time the RMI is attached during the serialization process of the network. This parameter can be either of the following flags:

- PREATTACH: This flag attaches the RMI before game data serialization.

- POSTATTACH: This flag attaches the RMI after game data serialization.

- NOATTACH: This flag is used when it is not important if the RMI is attached before or after the game data serialization.

- FAST: This flag performs an immediate transfer of the RMI without waiting for a frame update. This flag is very CPU intensive and should be avoided if possible.

The Net.Expose table we just added defines which functions will be exposed on the client and the server and will give us access to the following three subtables:

- allClients

- otherClients

- server

With these functions, we can now call functions either on the server or the clients. You can use the allClients subtable to call a function on all clients or the otherClients subtable to call it on all clients except the own client.

At this point, the entity table of our script should look as follows:

```
Testy = {
  Properties={
```

```
      fileModel = "",
      Physics = {
        bRigidBody=1,
        bRigidBodyActive = 1,
        Density = -1,
        Mass = -1,
      },
    Client = {},
    Server = {},

    Editor={
      Icon="User.bmp",
      ShowBounds = 1,
    },
  }
Net.Expose {
  Class = Testy,
  ClientMethods = {
    PrintLogOutput = { RELIABLE_UNORDERED, POST_ATTACH, STRING },
  },
  ServerMethods = {
    SvRequestLogOutput = { RELIABLE_UNORDERED, POST_ATTACH,
      STRING},
  },
  ServerProperties = {
  },
};
```

This defines our entity and its network exposure. With our latest updates, the rest of our script with all its functions should look as follows:

```
functionTesty.Server:OnInit()
  self:OnReset();
end;

functionTesty:OnReset()
  local props=self.Properties;
  if(not EmptyString(props.fileModel))then
    self:LoadObject(0,props.fileModel);
  end;
  EntityCommon.PhysicalizeRigid(self,0,props.Physics,0);
  self:DrawSlot(0, 1);
end;
```

```
functionTesty:OnPropertyChange()
  self:OnReset();
end;

functionTesty.Client:PrintLogOutput(text)
  Log(text);
end;

functionTesty.Client:OnHit(user)
  self.server:SvRequestLogOutput("My Text!");
end

functionTesty.Server:SvRequestLogOutput(text)
  self.allClients:PrintLogOutput(text);
end
```

With these functions added to our entity, everything should be ready to go and you can test the behavior in game mode. When the entity is being shot at, the OnHit() function will request the log output to be printed from the server. The server calls the actual function on all clients.

Using the state machine

CryENGINE provides simple state machine logic for Lua entities. This allows you to easily set up different states and create the behavior of a simple state machine. If you want to implement something similar to a switch that can be on or off, or a door that can be opened or closed, using the built-in state machine will do most of the work for you.

Not every entity needs to make use of this state machine logic, but for more complex entities, it is quite nice to have this extra bit of functionality built-in.

In order to add a state to an entity, you just need to list the names of all your states once within your main table so that the engine knows which states your entity has. This can be as many or as few as you need. Take a look at the following line of code:

```
States = {"SomeState", "AnotherState"},
```

Just like with any other state machine, only one state at a time can be active and there are specific functions to handle the transitions between the states. You need to add a state table to the script for each of your states, each containing the functions for entering, updating, and leaving the state. For the `Testy` entity that we have used in our examples so far, the state table would look like the following:

```
Testy.Server.SomeState=
{
  OnBeginState = function( self )
    end,
  OnUpdate = function(self, dt)
    end,
  OnEndState = function( self )
    end,
}
```

The table called `SomeState` is defined in the script and the state transition functions are added within it. Once you have one or more of those states defined in your script, you can use the following functions to build your state transition logic:

```
Entity.GetState(entity)
Entity.GotoState(entity, state)
```

With these two functions, you can get the current state of an entity and set it to transition to a new state. To set our entity to start in the state `SomeState`, for example, we could add the following line to our `OnInit()` function:

```
self:GotoState("SomeState");
```

Using script binds

The CryENGINE Lua script implementation provides many very useful script binds. A script bind is basically a C++ engine function that has been exposed to Lua. This way, you can have access to pretty much any CryENGINE functionality in your Lua scripts. Many script binds are already available, for example, to start sounds, animations, or to send commands to the AI system. You can also easily expose more functionalities by adding your own script binds. Exposing and using script bind functions is rather easy and straightforward.

Calling script binds

Using a script bind is quite easy. Simply call the script bind as you would call any other Lua function. For example, the following code is a system script bind function that simply shuts down the engine:

```
System.Quit()
```

Apart from the function name, you will need to know the global namespace for the script bind you want to call. In the aforementioned example, it is System. The name of the namespace is defined by the C++ code that defines and exposes the script bind.

There are hundreds of different script binds available for all kinds of different systems of CryENGINE. The official CryENGINE documentation provides an overview and description of all available script binds.

Creating new script binds

A new C++ script bind can be created easily by adding it to the according C++ file. There are different places for you to create the new script bind. Depending on what you want to add, you can choose different files to define your script bind. A generic game-related script bind could, for example, be placed in ../CryGameSDK/GameFiles/ScriptBind_Game.h. You can simply add your script bind declaration in the file. Let's say you want to add a simple function that draws some text on the screen. You could add the following line of code:

```
intDrawSomeText(IFunctionHandler*pH,constchar*someText);
```

Then, you can go ahead and implement the function in CryGameSDK/GameFiles/ScriptBind_Game.cpp.

This would look something like the following code snippet:

```
intCScriptBind_Game::DrawSomeText(IFunctionHandler *pH,
constcharsomeText)
{

//Do something

return pH->EndFunction(1);
}
```

With the function implementation done, we just have to add one more thing. We have to add the actual script bind exposure to Lua. This is also done in `CryGameSDK/GameFiles/ScriptBind_Game.cpp`. The code for this looks like the following code snippet:

```
SCRIPT_REG_TEMPLFUNC(DrawSomeText, "string");
```

With this new function added and the registration as a script bind complete, the code can now be compiled. Then, the new script bind can be used in your Lua scripts as shown in the following line of code:

```
Game.DrawSomeText("My Text");
```

Adding a new script bind is always a good choice when more complex and possibly expensive functionality is needed. Executing this code in C++ is usually more efficient and much faster than doing it within the Lua scripts.

Using engine callbacks

The Lua entities are notified of system and entity events through the engine callback functions. These are optional functions within your Lua entity that will be called automatically. An example of this is the `OnUsed()` function, which is called when the player tries to use your entity.

There are a lot of Lua script callbacks defined in CryENGINE that allow you to work more efficiently with your scripts. We have used some of the basic engine callbacks, such as the following, in our example script:

- `OnReset`
- `OnPropertyChange`
- `OnInit`

These three callbacks, for example, are used in almost every Lua entity and make your life a lot easier. `OnReset`, for example, is called automatically every time the script is reloaded, while `OnPropertyChange` is called whenever you change one of the entity's properties in Sandbox. The `OnInit` callback is triggered when the actual game is started or you jump into game mode in Sandbox. Utilizing these callbacks makes it very easy to set up and control your entity behavior.

The official CryENGINE documentation provides an overview of all available script callbacks, and it is available at `http://freesdk.crydev.net/display/SDKDOC5/Callback+References`.

The use of those callbacks makes it a lot easier to build functional and versatile Lua entities.

Using the Lua debugger

Although debugging a Lua script is a bit easier than debugging the C++ code, it can sometimes be useful to have the ability to set breakpoints and step through the script. This is where the Lua debugger comes in. This very useful tool is easy to overlook since it is very well hidden, without any user interface that would let you find it.

The Lua debugger can be operated using the following two console commands:

- `lua_debugger`
- `lua_debugger_show`

While `lua_debugger` will enable the debugger, `lua_debugger_show` will open the debugger window to let you have a closer look at things. Take a look at the following screenshot:

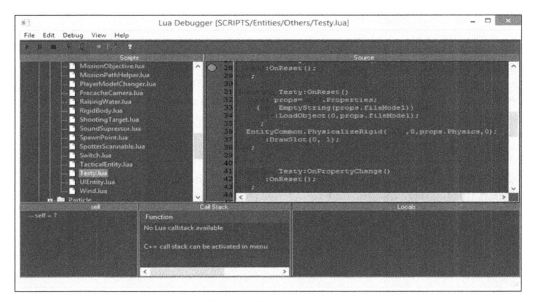

The Lua debugger window

Using the Lua debugger is very similar to using any other debugger such as Visual Studio. When the debugger is active, it allows you to set breakpoints, trace points, step through your script, and look at the content of your variables more closely. The Lua debugger is available in both Sandbox and your actual CryENGINE executable.

The **Scripts** window on the left-hand side provides you with an overview of all entity scripts. If we want to debug our newly made entity, we can select it in this window and set breakpoints according to our needs.

For example, to debug the text output function we added, we have to perform the following steps:

1. Enter game mode in either Sandbox or Launcher.

2. Open the console and type `lua_debugger_show`.

3. In the **Scripts** section of the debugger window, navigate to **Scripts | Others | Testy.lua** and double-click on the filename to select it.

4. Click on the line number next to the line containing the log output to set a breakpoint.

5. Click on the **Play** button in the top-left corner of the debugger window.

```
48    ;
49
50          Testy.Client:PrintLogOutput(text)
51    Log(text);
52    ;
53
```

A breakpoint has been set in the Lua debugger

After clicking on the **Play** button in the debugger window, the game will continue and you can go ahead and shoot your entity with any weapon. Once the hit is registered and our function is called, the debugger window will open again after it hits the breakpoint.

Now, you can use the information provided in the lower section of the debugger window to take a closer look at a potential problem. The debugger provides you with a Lua call stack and the possibility to look at all the values of your entity table. Although only the Lua callstack is shown and not the full C++ callstack, the debugger can provide you with a lot of information.

Once you are done with a specific breakpoint, you can either remove it or click on the **Play** button again to continue.

You can set and remove breakpoints by clicking on a line number in the Lua debugger window.

In addition to the debugger window user interface, the system provides you with a few shortcuts to make things simpler. You can use the following keys to control the Lua debugger:

*   *F5* to continue
*   *F9* to toggle breakpoint

- *F10* to step over
- *F11* to step into

All this functionality will make your life a bit easier when you have to hunt down difficult problems in your Lua scripts. Remember that you can also use the Lua debugger in your actual game runtime, should you need to investigate a problem that occurred while the game was running in pure game mode.

Summary

After learning all about the visual scripting tool flow graph in *Chapter 3, Building Complex Flow Graph Logic*, in this chapter, we took a close look at CryENGINE's Lua script implementation. We talked about the capabilities of the Lua script and looked at the way it is implemented and used in CryENGINE. You learned how to create a new Lua entity from scratch, add functionality to it, and make it network-ready.

The next chapter will be all about animating characters in the engine. We will go through all the steps necessary to get your own character in the game set up and fully animated. We will also talk about the new CryMannequin animation system.

7
Animating Characters

The ideal animation system is both easy to use and at the same time offers a wide range of powerful features. While this is not necessarily an oxymoron, such a perfect animation system is hard to find.

To meet the requirements of modern AAA games, animation systems have to have a certain degree of complexity to offer all the functionalities that are needed. The trade-off of this is that these systems demand a bit of technical expertise from the user.

In this chapter, we will cover the following topics:

- CryMannequin's animation system
- Extending the state machine
- Playing animation without CryMannequin

The CryENGINE animation system

When talking about the animation system in CryENGINE 3, or almost any animation system in general, it makes sense to divide it into a high-level and a low-level system. A more detailed subdivision is possible, of course, but is not necessary for the topics covered in this chapter.

The low-level system is responsible for blending the individual keys together for all animations that are currently running on a character. The components of the low-level system work directly on the character's skeleton. The code for this system is highly optimized for performance and should not be modified without proper technical knowledge.

This is where the Look IK is applied; the Aim Poses are blended together which makes the character look and aim in the direction he or she is supposed to. Then, the blendspace or locomotion groups are evaluated — these blend together various walk and run animations of the character to match his or her animation with the speed, slope, and angular velocity of the entity movement. This is also where the command buffer is implemented and the PoseModifiers are managed; these handle all the functionalities I just spoke about. Almost all the code related to the low-level animation system sits in the CryAnimation DLL. Most users will never touch this part of the animation system. If you intend to modify and extend the core of the animation system, you will require access to the full source code of the engine. Take a look at the following screenshot which displays a character's animation:

Using the animation system the right way can make your character come alive

The high-level animation system includes everything that is used to *control* the low-level system. This includes tools and systems to start animations on a character, such as **TrackView**, the **FlowGraph** nodes, or an animation selection logic. In CryENGINE 3, the high-level animation system is mostly handled by a state machine and the so-called CryMannequin system.

Introducing CryMannequin

CryENGINE 3.5 obsoleted the previously used high-level animation system, the Animation Graph. It was replaced with the CryMannequin system (or simply called Mannequin). These two systems are quite different in terms of their setup, usage, and the tasks that they perform; therefore, unfortunately, there is no simple way of converting an Animation Graph setup that is older than Version 3.5 into an equivalent CryMannequin setup. If you upgrade from Version 3.4.x to 3.5.x in the middle of a project, you will have to create a new animation setup for your game.

Because the systems are so different, it makes sense to explain what CryMannequin is and what it does. This should be interesting even for readers who have experience with the Animation Graph from previous versions of CryENGINE.

The official documentation includes tutorials that cover how to create a Mannequin setup for a new character, but there seems to be a lack of a good and easy-to-understand explanation of the basics of the system. This has caused confusion and many open questions in regards to the system. This chapter will attempt to fill this gap without repeating the material already covered in the official documentation.

Splitting up the game and animation logic

CryMannequin allows the separation of the game and animation logic. This means that the code that controls the game logic—for example, moving the character, shooting, jumping, punching, and so on—does not directly call into the low-level animation system to start a specific animation on a character. Instead, it calls upon CryMannequin with the information of what kind of animation to play. CryMannequin then takes care of picking the right animation(s).

This might seem unintuitive at first, because it is an *indirect* system, but it makes for a much cleaner game logic code. The following are a couple of examples of this process:

- If the code that makes the player move would also have to start the animations, it would need to know exactly which animations the character has available for running and walking, what their names are, and how to blend them together. As the same code needs to take care of different character types with different animations, this would quickly become a messy endeavor. Instead, the code that takes care of the movement should simply tell the high-level animation system that the character is moving.

- Idle breaks are another example of this. Idle breaks are those animations that play after the character has been standing still for a few moments. Usually, they are randomly picked variations of actions such as looking around, scratching various body parts, yawning, and so on. Their purpose is to make a character look more alive when not moving.

The movement controller of a character can notify the high-level animation system that the character is now standing still, in other words, idling. But it doesn't need to take care of starting idle break animations. Each character will have a different amount of idle breaks, and they will have different animation names. Hardcoding the animation names inside the code that handles movement is therefore unwise.

All in all, it makes sense to keep the game logic and the animation logic separate. Your character's list of animations will grow and change over time; in early development especially, a character will commonly not have as many animations available, because they are still being created. If you start hardcoding animation names into your source code, you are headed for much grief down the road.

Understanding CryMannequin's purpose

As mentioned before, CryMannequin is a high-level animation system. As such, its main task is selecting, starting, and transitioning animations so that the game logic doesn't have to do it. It acts as an intermediate layer between the game logic and the low-level animation system. In a nutshell, it knows what animations are available for a character and how to play them.

CryMannequin abstracts the starting and stopping of animations for the game logic. The different functions of CryMannequin are best explained individually and with examples. This will be done in the next few sections.

Selecting animations

Before Mannequin can start an animation, it needs to make the decision of choosing which animation to play. In other words, it needs to *select* an animation.

Let's continue with the previous example of the character's movement. The game logic knows that the player is moving forward, for example, at a running speed; however, instead of starting an animation by name, the movement controller tells CryMannequin to start a run.

Terminology

In this example, the game logic tells CryMannequin to start the Fragment ID called Run. However, Fragments and Fragment IDs will be explained in more detail later in this chapter.

CryMannequin knows that the character in our example has a range of different run animations available. They are divided depending on what weapon the character is holding and what stance he is in, for example, stealth or combat mode. All the animations look slightly different in terms of arms and body posture, so it is important to pick the right one.

The piece of information that indicates which weapon is currently selected is provided by the item system. The information about the current stance of the player is provided by the stance system. CryMannequin will take all of this data into account, select the correct animation, and start it as shown in the following diagram:

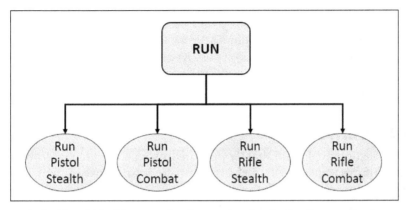

CryMannequin decides which of the run animations to play after the Run Fragment has been requested

The code handling the movement never sees or knows about the exact animation that was chosen to play. It can focus solely on its task to move the character around.

Now let's play the same scenario again for a different character. The game logic tells CryMannequin to run. However, this particular character only has a single run animation available. CryMannequin will select and play it, regardless of the currently selected weapon or stance, as shown in the following diagram:

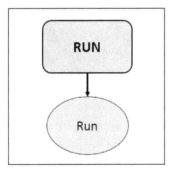

Not all characters have the same animations available

In both scenarios, the code that runs the game logic is exactly the same. It doesn't need to concern itself with animation names or selection, as that is kept separate from it. On the CryMannequin side, the animation setup for characters can be totally different and as simple or complex as you want or need it to be.

It is important to understand that the top-level selection logic is *not* handled in CryMannequin. The game logic selects the Run Fragment ID, and CryMannequin only chooses which version of the run to play. This is different from the Animation Graph in prior CryENGINE versions, which took care of the entire selection logic.

Starting animations

The previous section explained that CryMannequin selects the animation to play based on the information provided by the game logic and the different game systems. In the examples used so far, the animations were single looping full-body animations, such as a run or an idle. However, CryMannequin can handle much more complicated animations. In fact, this is where its main strength lies.

At first, we need to clarify the terminology. In the previous sections, we always talked about animations; however, instead of individual animations, CryMannequin deals with so-called Fragments and Fragment IDs. A Fragment is simply a container for an animation sequence. Aside from one or more animation names to play, it also contains information on how to play these animations. In its simplest form, a Fragment might just be a single looping animation as in our previous examples. Take a look at the following diagram:

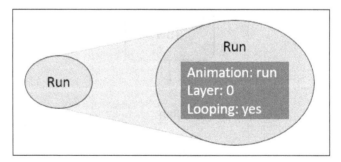

A Fragment is more than just an animation name

The preceding diagram shows an example of what other forms of data a Fragment can hold. Keep in mind that this is a simplification; in fact, a Fragment can be much more complex than this.

As an advanced user, you will most likely have some experience with **TrackView**. A CryMannequin Fragment is very much like a **TrackView** sequence. Using it, you can set up animations on a timeline and on several layers. For the player character, you can even specify different animations for the first-person and third-person modes. Take a look at the following screenshot:

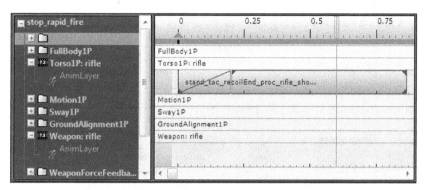

A Fragment offers you a timeline and multiple animation layers

With the power of a timeline and access to the various animation layers at your fingertips, you can easily set up complex animation sequences. Imagine that you want to set up a Smoking Fragment. If so, the first animation in the sequence would have the character light a cigarette. Then, you would add in an animation of the character actually smoking the cigarette and playing it on loop. You can crop the animations, crossfade them, and even change their playback speed. The entire sequence will be stored inside the Fragment and played back when the Fragment is started. It is this freedom that makes CryMannequin quite a powerful tool.

It is important to understand that no matter how simple or complex the setup of your Fragments is, the selection of the game logic side always stays the same. The Movement Controller will make the decision of putting the character in Run, regardless of what the Fragment that CryMannequin will ultimately select looks like.

Fragments, Fragment IDs, and Tags

The previous sections have theoretically explained how CryMannequin works in principle and introduced the concept of Fragments. It is important to understand these concepts before moving on. This section will introduce Fragment IDs and Tags, and explain how these work together.

First, let's look at some terminologies. In the previous examples, the movement-controlling code of the character would ask CryMannequin to start a Run action, and that would then lead to a Fragment being selected and its animation sequence being played. This Run action is actually called a Fragment ID. The name can be misleading as it suggests that a Fragment ID is merely an identifier for a Fragment. This is not the case. A Fragment ID is a container that holds multiple Fragments of the same type. Take a look at the following diagram:

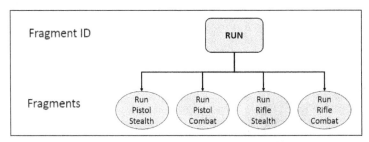

This example RUN Fragment ID contains four Fragments

The game logic will only ever ask CryMannequin to start Fragment IDs, not individual Fragments. The decision of choosing which Fragment to pick from the Fragment ID is up to CryMannequin (if there is more than one available).

For Animation Graph users

A Fragment ID corresponds most to the Animation Graph concept of a state. It is not an exact match, but a state could contain one or more animations and be parameterized by things such as an item or stance.

The decision of which Fragment to pick is made based on the additional information provided by the various game systems, for example, the **item** system, the **vehicle** system, or the **Stance** system. This information is compared with the selection criterion that is set up on the Fragments.

This additional information is stored in the so-called Tags. The Tags variables are set from game systems. There is, for example, a Tag called **Stance**, which will be filled at runtime by the stance system with the name of the stance that the character is currently in.

Fragments have a setup for which Tag values they should match with. A fragment that contains an animation sequence for a kneeling idle action would, for example, have its **Stance** Tag set to **Crouch**; it would most likely be one of the many fragments inside the Fragment ID `Idle`. The Fragment ID will most likely contain more fragments to cover the other stances as well. You can see which Tag values a Fragment requires by double-clicking on it in **Mannequin Editor**. The Tags will appear on the left-hand side of the timeline, as shown in the following screenshot:

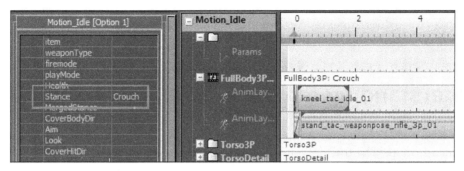

A screenshot of the Fragment handling the crouching stance inside the Fragment ID Idle

For Animation Graph users

The Tags work similar to the Inputs used in the Animation Graph, but unlike that system, they do not have a priority. Tags are also not limited in number like the Inputs were.

Extending the state machine

As mentioned earlier, CryMannequin can only choose which Fragment to start within a Fragment ID. The game logic decides which Fragment ID to start. This is done in a state machine inside the game code.

Not all games need to extend this state machine, as it already offers states for a large range of different actions such as locomoting, jumping and sliding, and even zip lining and ledge grabbing. If your game needs no new states, you will only need to modify or exchange the Fragments inside the existing Fragment IDs.

While there are multiple tutorials that cover the setup of CryMannequin and the creation of new Fragment IDs, Tags, and Fragments, there is very little written on the state machine that represents the high-level selection logic. This section will explain how to extend the state machine and add (and trigger) a new state that will start a newly added CryMannequin Fragment ID.

 At the time of this writing, the only way to add new states to the state machine is through the C++ source code. All of the code developed in this chapter can be used in both the full version and the free SDK version of CryENGINE.

Understanding the state machine hierarchy

The state machine is implemented and hardcoded inside the GameSDK DLL. Currently, the SDK ships with three top-level states, which have more states nested underneath them. The three top-level states are `Movement`, `Linked`, and `Animation`.

The **Animation** state contains states that typically control the player's movement and position via the animation, such as cutscenes, object interactions, or zip lining. The **Linked** state contains all those cases where the character is attached to another object, for example, a vehicle.

The **Movement** state houses everything else; most importantly, locomotion of any kind, including sliding and swimming. It contains by far the most substates out of the three.

 The Version 3.5.4 release of CryENGINE accidentally shipped without the `PlayerStateAnimationControlled.cpp` file. This file contains the implementation of the `Animation` state. This has been fixed with the Version 3.5.6 release.

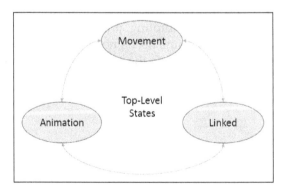

The main top-level states of the default CryENGINE SDK state machine

As the diagram shows, each state can transition to one of the other two states (or from and to a substate within them). The transition logic is handled by the states themselves. Like any regular state machine, the states will receive events. Depending on the event and the circumstances, the state might then decide to switch to a different state.

For example, consider that a character is walking. This is a substate of the **Movement** state. A cutscene is then triggered, and this event is sent to the currently active state. As a result, the **Movement** state, which contains the walking state, is left and the cutscene substate inside **Animation** is started. All substates of a state will automatically be exited when the parent state is left.

As in every state machine, triggers can cause a transition from the current state into a new one. In the Mannequin state machine, these triggers are sent in the form of player state events. These could be anything, say, a player entering a ladder or starting to slide. The events are defined in the `EPlayerStateEvent` enum. It is important to know that not all player state events need to trigger a transition to a new state. State events are also sent when you enter or leave a state.

Each state has a function that handles the player state events; thus, each state can decide whether it is time to switch to a different state. Since the states are nested, all states in the hierarchy above receive the events as well and can react to them.

An example in the SDK code where this is demonstrated is the **Movement Root** state. In its main function, `CPlayerStateMovement::MovementRoot()`, it will trigger the transition to the **Ladder** state as soon as it receives the event `PLAYER_EVENT_LADDER`. The substates **Swim** and **Run** do not need to handle this event themselves, and you will not find any code for them in their implementations. Take a look at the following diagram:

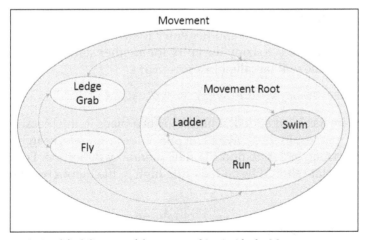

A simplified diagram of the state machine inside the Movement state

The advantage of this is that not every state needs to know about every other state and when to transition to them. They can simply let one of their parents take care of it. Each substate inside **Movement**, for example, would not need to take care of transitioning to states inside **Animation** or **Linked**. The top-level state would take care of this. Thus, it is important to choose the right position in the hierarchy for your new state.

The states themselves often do more than just start a CryMannequin Fragment ID, as they also contain some game logic. This chapter will only focus on the animation aspect of the states. The next section will explain step-by-step how to add a new state into the state machine and have it trigger a new CryMannequin Fragment ID.

 All code from the next section can be downloaded from the Packt website. You can simply copy and paste the functions into the appropriate files.

Creating a new state

In almost all cases, the new state you wish to create will fall into one of the three main categories: Movement, Animation, and Linked. Therefore, it is usually not necessary to create a new top-level state. In this section, we will add a new state inside Movement.

The file that contains the state machine for this top-level state is called PlayerStateMovement.cpp and can be found in the GameSDK DLL. The state machine implementation is heavily templated and uses a lot of macros. This makes adding new states very simple.

The first step is to create a new state within the class. This needs to be done before it can be placed in the hierarchy. To do so, you need to go into the constructor of CPlayerStateMovement and add another entry to the state declarations in there. The fastest way to do this is to copy the entry for another state. In the following code example, the new state will be called ExampleState:

```
DECLARE_STATE_CLASS_ADD(CPlayer, ExampleState );
```

Now that the state has been added, it needs to get a place in the hierarchy. This is also done using macros. In the PlayerStateMovement.cpp file, search for the string DEFINE_STATE_CLASS_BEGIN to find the state hierarchy definition. For the next example, the new state should be added quite high in the hierarchy, right below the root level:

```
DEFINE_STATE_CLASS_ADD(CPlayer, CPlayerStateMovement,
  ExampleState, Root )
```

The new state `ExampleState` has now been added to the state machine. However, your code will not yet compile because the implementation of the state is missing. Every state needs to have a function that handles the events that are being sent to the state machine. To create such an implementation for `ExampleState`, a new function has to be added into `CPlayerStateMovement`, as shown in the following line of code:

```
onstCPlayerStateMovement::TStateIndexCPlayerStateMovement
::ExampleState( CPlayer& player, constSStateEvent& event )
```

An implementation for this exists for every state in the hierarchy. This function receives the state events and can decide whether the system should transition to a new state. Whether a state change should occur or not is coded into the return value of the function. If your state decides to change to a new state, it would return the ID of the state it wants to switch to. If it wants to do nothing, the function would return the predefined value, `State_Continue`. Note that a state change might still happen if one of the parent states of your state decides to switch to a different state.

For `ExampleState`, this function can be quite small and simple. It won't deal with triggering transitions to other states at all and will let the parent states take care of handling the player state events. Thus, it will ignore most of the events it receives. All it is supposed to do for the next example is to trigger a CryMannequin Fragment ID.

Every state will receive an event when it is being entered or exited. To trigger the Fragment ID, `ExampleState` will listen to the entering event and react to it. In the next code, it will start a Fragment ID with the name `ExampleFragmentID`. Make sure to exchange this name with the name of a valid Fragment ID you have created:

```
constCPlayerStateMovement::TStateIndexCPlayerStateMovement::
ExampleState( CPlayer& player, constSStateEvent& event )
{
constEPlayerStateEventeventID = static_cast
  <EPlayerStateEvent> (event.GetEventId());
switch(eventID )
{
case STATE_EVENT_ENTER:
{
IAnimatedCharacter* pAnimChar = player.GetAnimatedCharacter();
IActionController *pActCtrl = pAnimChar->GetActionController();
if (pActCtrl)
{
  constFragmentIDfragmentID = pActCtrl-
  >GetContext().controllerDef.m_fragmentIDs.Find
  ("ExampleFragmentID");
// Setting a high priority of 12
```

```
    IActionPtrpAction = new TAction<SAnimationContext>
      (12, fragmentID);
    pActCtrl->Queue(pAction);
  }
  break;
  }
  }
  returnState_Continue;
  }
```

The preceding code sample demonstrates how to retrieve the CryMannequin controller for the character and how to find and start a Fragment ID on it. There are no additional parameters required, since all the animation parameters are set up within the Fragments inside the Fragment ID.

When creating an action for the action controller, you will need to provide a priority. The controller uses this priority to disregard actions with lower priority if there is already one playing with a higher priority. This prevents systems from playing animations on a character that is dead or occupied with another animation so that it is not interrupted. You can see a list of predefined priorities as reference in the EPlayerActionPriority enum. The previous code sample sets the priority to 12 to ensure it is higher than everything else.

The state setup is now complete, and your code should compile without error at this point. However, the new state will not be called yet, because none of the other states are transitioning into it. This will be covered in the next section.

Triggering the new state

Now that we have a new state that will trigger our new Fragment ID, we need to make the state machine transition into the state. This section will demonstrate how this can be done by creating a new state event and linking it to an input. In your game or project, you will need to decide which circumstances should lead to your state being triggered. The code developed in this section can serve as a reference for your own game logic.

The first step is to create a new state event that will eventually trigger the transition to the new ExampleState. All state events can be found in the PlayerStateEvents.h file, which is located inside the GameSDK DLL. Open the file and find the EPlayerStateEvent enum. Add a new entry to the enum. Choose a name that matches the circumstances in which you wish to use it. For the next example, we will call it PLAYER_EVENT_EXAMPLEEVENT.

This event needs to be sent from somewhere, and the state machine needs to react to it. Let's take care of the latter first. Back in the file with the state machine implementation, `PlayerStateMovement.cpp`, find the function `MovementRoot()`. This function handles a lot of the events for the `Movement` state.

To trigger our new state, we need to return its state ID in this function. This will initiate the state transition in the state machine. Since everything is templated, the ID has been created automatically when the state was added in the previous section. To initiate the state transition, add a new `case` to the `switch` statement inside the function:

```
case PLAYER_EVENT_EXAMPLEEVENT:
    return State_ExampleState;
```

This will transition to the new state, and the state machine will ensure that the `enter` event is sent to `ExampleState`.

The last step is to send this event to the state machine. This can be done from any system you desire, and of course, even from within the state machine. For the next example, we will use an input event, the mouse wheel down to be exact, to trigger the event.

You can set up an entirely new `Input Action` if you want to. The exact steps of how this is done are explained in detail in *Chapter 2, Using the CryENGINE Input System – Keyboard, Mouse, and Game Controller*. Just so we do not repeat the information from that chapter, we will simply hijack an existing `Input Action` to trigger our new event here. In the `PlayerInput.cpp` file, find the following line of code:

```
ADD_HANDLER(previtem, OnActionSelectNextItem);
```

This will call the `OnActionSelectNextItem` function when `previtem` is received. This `Action` function is mapped to the mouse wheel. To hijack this, comment on the line and add your own function, `OnActionHijacked`, instead:

```
//ADD_HANDLER(previtem, OnActionSelectNextItem);
ADD_HANDLER(previtem, OnActionHijacked);
```

Now you need to create the `OnActionHijacked` function inside the `CPlayerInput` class and use it to trigger the `State` event. Note that you will need to declare the function in the header file as well. Take a look at the following code snippet:

```
boolCPlayerInput::OnActionHijacked
  ( EntityIdentityId, constActionId&actionId,
    intactivationMode, float value )
{
```

```
m_pPlayer->StateMachineHandleEventMovement(SStateEvent
  (PLAYER_EVENT_EXAMPLEEVENT) );
return false;
}
```

You can now compile the code and start the engine. Load a level and jump into the game. Depending on the Fragment you created, you might want to switch to the ThirdPerson camera mode so that you can see the body of your character. Scroll down using the mouse wheel to trigger your state event and then transition to the state you set up. You should see your Fragment ID playing.

Playing animations without CryMannequin

While CryMannequin will be the main system to select and play animations on your player and AI characters, there are other systems that you can use. This section will introduce what these are and which system to use for what purpose.

TrackView

The CryENGINE Sandbox Editor includes a tool called **TrackView**. This is a timeline tool that is commonly used to create full-blown cutscenes, but it can also be used for scripted sequences during gameplay.

It can be used to play animations on characters as well, and it offers access to several features of the animation system. It can play facial sequences as well (refer to *Chapter 4, Morphs and Bones – Creating a Facial Setup for Your Character*, for more information on this).

Multiple TrackView sequences can be active at the same time, and the player character doesn't need to be disabled. This means you can use a **TrackView** sequence to animate characters and objects in the background complete with particles, sounds, and so on.

As this is an advanced book, many readers will already have used the **TrackView** editor before. So, instead of giving a basic introduction to **TrackView**, this section will focus on how to use it more efficiently for animating characters during cutscenes and scripted sequences.

Multiple animation layers

Oftentimes, characters in a cutscene play back a single, long animation that spans the duration of the entire sequence. These animations are created in a **Motion Capture** session with actors, or hand-animated by animators.

This can be an expensive option that is cost prohibitive for smaller studios or projects that don't demand this level of effort for every character inside a cutscene. Instead of creating dedicated animations for every character in the sequence, you might simply use multiple, smaller game animations and blend them together.

To accommodate this, **TrackView** allows more than one animation track per character. This gives the user the option to play animations on multiple layers of the character and blend full- and partial-body animations together.

To add more animation tracks to an entity in **TrackView**, simply right-click on the entity again and navigate to **Add Track | Animation** from the pop-up menu:

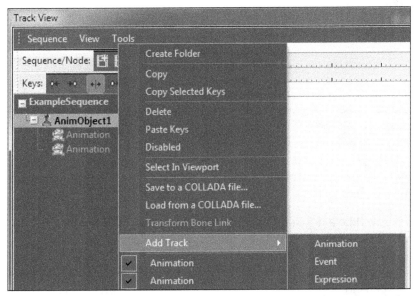

You are not limited to one single animation track in TrackView; simply add more through the menu.

The tracks are ordered from top to bottom. The first animation track will correspond to layer 0, the next to layer 1, and so on. This means that you should put full-body animations in the top-most track and partial-body animations into the tracks below. Every animation track will play on top of the ones above it.

Here is an example of a setup with three animation tracks. The top track plays a looping-idle animation. In the next track, it plays a partial-body-waving animation. The last one plays an additive on top of these animations to emulate breathing. Take a look at the following screenshot:

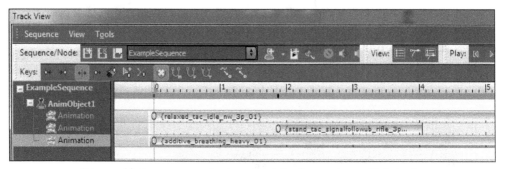

It is possible to access more than one animation layer using multiple tracks

There is another trick you should know when working with **TrackView** this way. To make blending between animations easier, **TrackView** extends the first and the last key of any animation indefinitely. In the preceding example, this behavior affects the second animation track. The animation in this track is not supposed to start until roughly around the 2 second mark, but the blending mechanism of **TrackView** causes the first frame of the animation to be active from the beginning of the sequence.

This can very well be a desired effect, as animations can be used as poses this way. However, if you don't want this to happen, you can place an empty key before and/ or after the animation to stop the layer. Be sure to enable **Blend Gap** on all keys so you get a nice fade-in and fade-out of your partial-body animation. Take a look at the following screenshot:

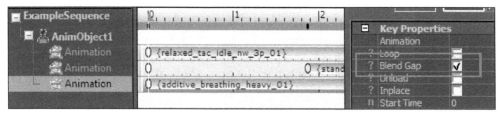

Use empty keys and Blend Gap to fade in and out of partial-body animations in TrackView

CryMannequin tracks

Apart from playing individual animation files, **TrackView** can also play back CryMannequin Fragments. This can save valuable setup time if a character is supposed to play an action in a cutscene that is already set up in CryMannequin.

To play back a Fragment, you need to add a **Mannequin** track to your entity. Note that this will only work with characters that have a CryMannequin setup loaded. `AnimObjects`, which are often used in **TrackView** sequences for performance purposes, do not have a CryMannequin setup by default. However, if you are using AI characters inside a cutscene, you have access to all of their loaded Fragments. Take a look at the following screenshot:

Specify the Fragment ID and the priority when using Mannequin tracks

When setting up keys in a **Mannequin** track in **TrackView**, you cannot specify the Fragment to play directly; instead, you will need to specify the Fragment ID. There is no direct way of copying a Fragment ID name; you will need to type it in manually.

The Fragment is played back through the Action Controller in the same way a state in the state machine plays back Fragments. Therefore, a priority check is performed. In almost all cases, you will want your cutscene to trump the game logic. Make sure to set the priority high enough so that the Fragment IDs started by the game logic won't override your Fragment playback.

 A work-around for the Fragment selection is to click on the **Edit ID...** button in **Mannequin Editor** and then copy the name of the desired Fragment ID into the clipboard. This avoids typos and is generally faster than manual typing.

Triggering animation from FlowGraph

FlowGraph can be used to start animations directly, without the CryMannequin or C++ code. The node for animation playback allows us to set various parameters on the animation. This option is mainly used for two purposes. One is to animate background characters or objects that are so simple that they do not even require a **TrackView** sequence. The other is to play single one-shot animations in reaction to gameplay.

CryMannequin can be used on non-player characters as well, as long as you create and load a Mannequin setup for them. This would require the implementation of a new entity type; however, at the time of this writing, the CryENGINE SDK does not ship with a sample entity that supports this.

The PlayAnimation node

The main node to play animations is called **PlayAnimation**, and it can be found in the **Animations** category. The following screenshot and the next few lines will explain the individual ports of the node:

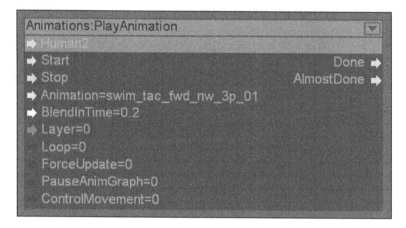

The **Start** and **Stop** inputs will trigger or end the animation. The **Animation** input needs to be filled with the name of an animation clip, not a CryMannequin Fragment ID. If you have already assigned a character to the node, clicking on the button next to the input field will present you with an animation list to choose from. The node can handle full-body, partial-body, and additive animations. **Aim** and **Look Poses** or other procedural animations will not work correctly however.

A long animation list can make it hard to find the right animation. Having the **Character Editor** open next to the **FlowGraph Editor** can make animation assignment a lot easier. Simply right-click on the animation that you would like and then select **Copy**. This will copy the animation name into the clipboard, allowing you to simply paste the name into the **FlowGraph** node.

The **BlendInTime** node allows you to set a time in seconds that is used to fade in the animation when it is started. The **Layer** input can be used to select a layer for the animation to play in. By default, the layer is 0. As a rule of thumb, you should always play full-body animations in layer 0 and partial-body animations in higher layers.

Setting the **ForceUpdate** input to true will set a special flag in the animation system that causes the animation to update every frame, even when the entity is not visible in the view. As an optimization, animations for entities that are not visible are not evaluated. This is a very important flag if your animation is supposed to move your character or object from its position.

The node has two output ports to signal that the animation has finished playing. The top port, **Done**, will be triggered when the animation has completely finished and is removed from the animation queue internally. If a new animation is started in the same layer and is crossfaded with the current one, this port will not be triggered until the animation has completely faded out.

The output port **AlmostDone** is triggered once the animation has been played 85 percent through. When chaining multiple animations together, this port can be used to start the next animation before this previous one has completely finished. This usually makes the crossfade result look nicer. However, keep in mind that this port might never trigger if the animation was aborted for any reason.

> Using this node with AI or player characters that have a CryMannequin setup is not recommended. There is currently no way of pausing the Mannequin system through **FlowGraph**, and the animation started through this node will most likely be overridden.

Other animation nodes

At the time of this writing, the SDK still ships with two additional **FlowGraph** nodes that were formerly used to trigger animations on characters. These nodes are called **AI:Anim** and **AI:AnimEx**. Due to the refactoring of the animation system, these nodes no longer work. These nodes might be removed or refactored in future releases, as they were used in conjunction with the now obsoleted Animation Graph system. Currently, these nodes are misleading, as they falsely let you select a CryMannequin Fragment ID to play an animation. However, the implementation of these nodes is not made to play back Mannequin Fragments. The use of these nodes will print an error message to the console.

The code

While it might seem unnecessary and cumbersome at first glance, there are plenty of reasons why you should start animations directly from code. You can opt to not use CryMannequin at all if you would rather code your animation logic completely on your own. Alternatively, you might want to write a system that triggers partial-body animations or additives depending on the gameplay in addition to the CryMannequin Fragments. In case you are using regular animations for your facial animations, you might implement a system to control these as well.

Whatever the reason, all the necessary code interfaces to start, stop, and manage animations are available inside the GameSDK DLL. This section will cover the steps needed to start an animation from code.

When you start an animation from the C++ code, you will need to know the exact name of the animation. You will also need to set all the parameters, such as what layer to play the animation on and how fast to blend it in.

All animations are started (and stopped) through the `ISkeletonAnim` interface. This interface can be queried for all characters, not just for players. So, you can use this to animate other entities as well.

This is a sample code that shows you how to retrieve the `ISkeletonAnim` interface. Note that depending on where you place this code, it might be enough to simply call `GetEntity()` to retrieve a pointer to the entity instead. Take a look at the following line of code:

```
IEntity* pEntity = m_pPlayer->GetEntity();
ICharacterInstance* pCharInst = pEntity->GetCharacter(0);
ISkeletonAnim* pSkelAnim = pCharInst->GetISkeletonAnim();
```

Armed with a pointer to the `ISkeletonAnim` interface and the name of the animation, you can start filling in the parameters you need to pass along with the call to the `StartAnimation()` function. The parameters need to be set into `struct`, which is passed as a parameter to the function. The `struct` parameter will set the default parameters for all options. The following code will modify the most common ones and start the animation:

```
CryCharAnimationParamsanimParams;
animParams.m_fPlaybackSpeed = 1.5f;
animParams.m_fTransTime = 2.0f;
animParams.m_nLayerID = 4;
animParams.m_nFlags = CA_LOOP_ANIMATION;
pSkelAnim->StartAnimation(animationName, animParams);
```

This code will start an animation in layer 4 with 1.5 times the normal playback speed. The animation will be crossfaded or blended in over 2 seconds and will be played on loop.

 When starting an animation by its name, the animation system needs to look into the animation, that is, in its internal list of animations to find its ID. If you repeatedly start the same animations, you should save the ID using GetAnimIDByName() and then use the function StartAnimationById() to start the animations instead.

Summary

This chapter showed you how the animation system of CryENGINE and CryMannequin work in detail. The concepts behind the system were explained, and it was demonstrated why this system can be very powerful.

You learned how to extend the state machine that controls the animation selection and were introduced to alternative methods of starting and handling animations.

The next chapter will introduce the Smart Object system and teach you how to use it to build a gameplay and enrich your AI characters' behaviors.

8
Mastering the Smart Objects System

CryENGINE ships with a very powerful AI and navigation system, a large number of Lua scripts, and even a visual scripting system, the flowgraph. All these systems allow you to create sophisticated content for your CryENGINE project. There is one additional system, however, which is more than useful when you are trying to create realistic and believable game environments: the SmartObject system. In this chapter, we will take a close look at CryENGINE's SmartObject system, how it works, and what it can be used for.

What are SmartObjects?

A SmartObject is a game object that is set up to interact with other game objects within the game's environment. These interactions between objects are defined by a set of classes and rules, which are set up by a level designer or programmer using Sandbox's SmartObject editor. Almost anything in a CryENGINE level can be a SmartObject. The SmartObject class or set of rules is completely independent from the actual object, its 3D model, or any other setup. An AI character can be a SmartObject, a vehicle, a weapon, or something as simple as a small rock on the ground. You can think of the SmartObject system as an easy way to script complex game behavior. And just like with the flowgraph, it can be used without any programming skills. The SmartObjects system allows you to set up game logic in a more systematic way than it would be possible by just using the flowgraph. The system has intentionally been designed to be used by level and game designers instead of programmers.

The following screenshot shows the SmartObjects editor:

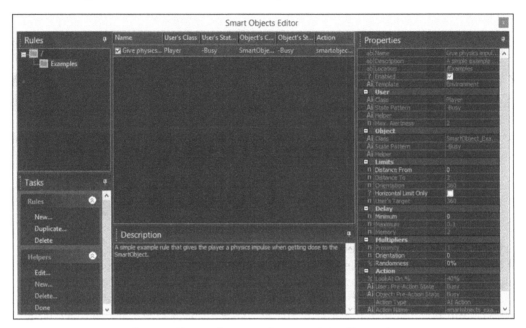

The SmartObjects editor is used to set up SmartObject rules

Where the Smart Objects system is used

The SmartObject system was added in CryENGINE 2 and has since then been used for many different purposes. Basically, you use the SmartObject system whenever you want to add more interactivity to your game environment. This can mean things like having AI characters react more naturally to their environment or certain objects reacting to the actions of the player.

Things typically achieved with the SmartObjects system are as follows:

- AI characters reacting to actions of the player
- Logic puzzles, interactive machines, and so on
- Interactive level backgrounds
- Scripted AI behaviors
- Specific navigational areas for AI characters to use

The system is very flexible and allows you to build all kinds of rules involving different types of classes.

Smart Objects categories

Each set of SmartObject rules can be categorized into one of the following three categories:

- Environmental
- Time based
- Navigational

Each category of SmartObject rules serves a different purpose. Depending on what kind of interaction you want to set up, your rules will fall into one of these three categories.

Environmental SmartObject

Environmental SmartObjects are used whenever you intend to set up an interaction between different objects in your game level. These might be regular objects as well as characters or vehicles. An AI character using a light switch SmartObject to switch a **Light** entity on and off would be an example of an environmental SmartObject. In this chapter, we will mainly focus on environmental SmartObjects and how to set them up.

A time-based SmartObject

Some SmartObject rules can be quite simple and not more than a simple timer might be needed to trigger them. In this case, a time-based SmartObject rule will be a good choice. Two AI characters standing next to each other for a certain amount of time could, for example, trigger a SmartObject action.

Navigational SmartObject

Navigational SmartObject rules are very powerful and can be used to set up and trigger animations in certain conditions. For example, you could set up a Smart Objects rule to have an enemy AI vault over a wall or kick in a door. In the games of the Crysis series, for example, whenever you see an enemy soldier sliding into cover or kicking in a door, it is most likely that SmartObjects have been used to achieve this.

The concept of the SmartObject system

The basic concept of the SmartObject system is quite simple and straightforward. You set up certain classes and states and then define one or more rules, which determine how the classes should interact with each other.

The main elements of the system are classes, states, rules, and actions:

- **A SmartObject class**: This defines a type of SmartObject
- **A SmartObject state**: This defines what state a SmartObject is currently in
- **A SmartObject rule**: This defines the interaction of the SmartObject classes
- **A SmartObject action**: This is executed when all the conditions of a rule are met

[A SmartObject rule takes the states of the SmartObject classes into account to decide what action is to be performed once all the conditions are met.]

All SmartObject rules work pretty much the same way. A new rule is defined by picking different classes to interact with each other, depending on their state. When all conditions are met, an action will be executed as seen in the following figure. We will have a closer look at what type of actions can be executed later in this chapter.

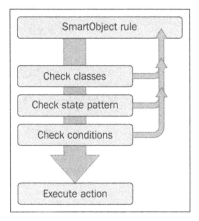

The SmartObjects editor

All SmartObject work is done in Sandbox using the Smart Objects editor, which has been integrated into the Sandbox toolkit. Like many of the other tools included in Sandbox, the **Smart Objects Editor** can be found by navigating to **View | OpenViewPane**.

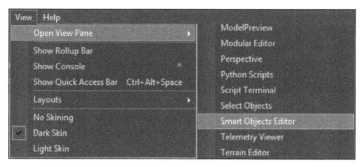

The SmartObjects editor can be found in the View menu

This SmartObject editor allows you to create new rules, classes, and actions. Before we get started, let's have a look at how the editor is laid out.

The Window layout of the SmartObject editor

There are three different areas within the SmartObjects editor window. Just like with any other window in Sandbox, you can undock and rearrange the individual windows. The default layout, however, should work well for the examples we are about to see in this chapter.

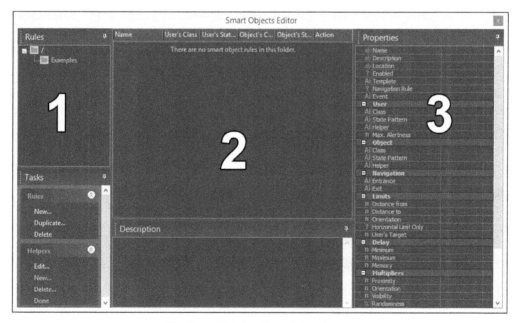

The SmartObjects editor window layout

The three important parts of the **Smart Objects Editor** window are:

- The **Rules** and **Tasks** window
- The **Rules List** window
- The Rule **Properties** window

Before we go ahead, let's have a look at what information and control is provided with each window.

The Rules and Tasks windows

The left side of the editor window contains the **Rules** and **Tasks** windows. While the **Rules** window provides an overview of all existing rules, the **Tasks** window contains all the main controls to create, edit, or delete new rules. The **Rules** window displays all existing rules in a tree view and allows you to organize your rules in subfolders. When a folder is selected in this window, the **Rules List** window will be updated with information about the rules in the selected folder.

The Rules List window

The rules list can be found in the center of the **Smart Objects Editor** window. This is where you get an overview of all rules in the selected folder and the details of the rules. You can click on the rules to enable/disable them or jump directly to the action the rule is executing.

The **Rules List** window displays a summary of the selected rule in an easy-to-read way. The specific properties of a rule are not displayed in the the **Rules List** window, however, the basic information displayed allows you to get a good overview of how the selected rule is working.

The Rule Properties window

All the way on the right side, you can find the Rule **Properties** window. Here you get a detailed listing of all the properties, which have been set up for the rule. Depending on the type of the selected rule, the Rule **Properties** window will display a different set of properties. We will go over the details of the specific properties later in this chapter in the *Creating a new SmartObject rule* section.

The SmartObject library

SmartObjects are stored in a library inside your CryENGINE folder and can be shared and exported just like other libraries in the engine. The information displayed in the **Rules** and **Tasks** windows is being read from the SmartObject library file and rule changes are saved in it after changes have been made. The SmartObject library file can be found at `..\GameSDK\Libs\SmartObjects.xml`.

All the rules are stored in a relatively simple XML format. When working with the SmartObjects system, it is important to check out the library file first and make sure it can be written to. The `..\GameSDK\Libs\..` folder also contains a SmartObjects folder, which holds a file called `SOTemplates.xml`. This file contains all the predefined templates for the rule types. If you want to add a new SmartObject template to support a new type of rule, you can use this file for it. Before we go ahead, make sure the SmartObject library file is checked out and not write protected.

SmartObject rules are not stored in your level file but in an external XML file located in the `..\GameSDK\Libs\` directory. The `SmartObjects.xml` file has to be writable in order to make changes to the SmartObject rules.

Creating a new SmartObject rule

With the SmartObject library file now writable, we can go ahead and add a new rule. For this example, we will create a new rule to use on an AI character and several environment objects. Let's build a *mechanic* AI using the SmartObject system.

Our goal for this example of a mechanic AI is to build a simple SmartObject behavior, which will control an AI character so that it detects broken things in its environment and automatically approaches and repairs them. This behavior can then be extended and improved with more sophisticated game logic, but for this example, we will keep things simple. We will build our mechanic AI by creating new classes, states, and a rule to trigger the according actions.

To achieve this, we need to perform the following steps:

1. Prepare a level, character, and environment objects for our example.
2. Create a new rule.
3. Create new classes for the mechanic and the things he is supposed to repair.
4. Create new states for the mechanic and the things he is supposed to repair.

5. Create a state pattern to trigger the action, taking into account the classes and states.

6. Create an action to repair the broken things.

Preparing the level

For our example, we will need to create a basic CryENGINE level. It should contain a basic terrain, a character, and some environment objects, such as machines our mechanic can repair later. One of the great things about SmartObjects is that they are really independent from a level. We will need a level, of course, so we can test the behavior properly but SmartObject rules will work in any level and environment.

Let's start by creating a new level in Sandbox. Nothing fancy, just some empty terrain with an AI navigation mesh, a character, and some objects. You can later improve the level of course or take the SmartObject rules and use them in your own levels.

A simple level with an AI character and some objects will do for our example

For the setup shown in the preceding screenshot, a small new level has been created. The following entities have been placed in the level:

- An AI Navigation area
- An AI Character with default settings
- Three barrels using the DestroyableObject class

To make sure the level and setup work, let's go through it step-by-step:

1. Create a new small level with a size of 256 x 256 at 1 m resolution and create a basic terrain so that objects can be placed on it.

2. Place an AI navigation area encompassing the area you intend to use to set up the objects in.

3. In the **Rollup Bar**, go to **Entity | AI | Characters** and place a **Human** character in the level.

4. Change the **Faction** property of the character to **Players** so the AI won't be hostile towards you when you enter the game mode.

5. In the **Rollup Bar**, go to **Entity | Physics** and place a **DestroyableObject** in the level.

This is all we will need for our example for now. After you place all the objects, make sure you save your CryENGINE level.

We placed three DestroyableObjects in the level, which will act as things for our mechanic to repair. Before we go ahead and set up any SmartObject rules, let's customize the DestroyableObjects a bit.

Adjust the following properties of the DestroyableObject:

- **Explosion.Pressure** to 0
- **Explosion.Damage** to 0
- **Health.MaxHealth** to 1

These changes will make sure that our AI won't get hurt or killed when we shoot our DestroyableObjects to break them. The default object used by the DestroyableObject is a breakable barrel. You can, however, exchange the 3D model and use any other asset if you like. The type of 3D model used does not affect the behavior of the entity. We could, for example, replace the 3D model with an actual machine later on, which can break down properly and has animations for breaking / being repaired.

Creating the SmartObject rule

Now that we have set up our level and the objects we need, we are ready to go ahead and start building some game logic.

Next up is creating the SmartObject classes we need for our mechanic and the things he is supposed to repair. New classes can easily be created in the SmartObjects editor by performing the following steps:

1. In the **Tasks** window in the SmartObject window, click on **Rules/New** to open the template selection dialog box.

2. In the SmartObject templates dialog box, select the **Environment** template and click on **OK**.

3. In the now open rule creation dialog box, type `Mechanic` in the **Rule name** textbox.

4. Optionally, add a description in the **Description** textbox.

5. Click on **OK** to create the new rule.

That is all that is needed to create a new rule. Now, we have a new rule called **Mechanic**, which is based on the **Environment** template. Our new rule should look like the following screenshot:

Name	User's Class	User's State Pattern	Object's Class	Object's State Pattern	Action
☑ Mechanic	Actor	-Busy		-Busy	

A new SmartObjects rule that has not been not customized yet

We are now ready to set up the classes for our mechanic and other objects.

Creating the SmartObject classes

For our example, we will just need two different classes. One for our mechanic and one for the objects he is supposed to repair. To create the new classes, perform the following steps:

1. Select the newly created **Mechanic** rule in the **Rules List** window of the SmartObject editor.

2. In the Rules **Properties** window, find the **User** tab and click on **Class**.

3. Click on the browse icon of the **Class** property to open the class selection dialog box.

⊟	**User**	
Ai	Class	Actor
Ai	State Pattern	-Busy
Ai	Helper	
n	Max. Alertness	2

The Class property of the SmartObject rule

The class selection dialog box lets us create and edit SmartObject classes. For our example, we can place our classes inside the example folder. You can always change the folder structure or move your rules to a different folder.

The class selection dialog box

Click on the **/Examples** folder and then the **New** button to create a new class. Enter a name for the class in the **New Class** dialog box which opens up. We can call this class MechanicGuy, since it will be used for the AI going around and repairing things. You can also add an optional description for this class if you like.

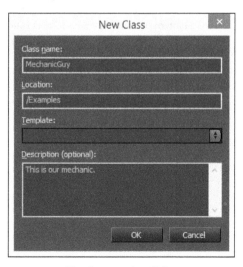

The class creation dialog

Now, we have a new class we can use in our example. Let's go ahead and create another class for the objects to be repaired. Follow the preceding steps to create another class called `Machine`. Those two classes are all we need to build our example.

Creating the SmartObject states

Next up is creating the states that will be used to determine when SmartObject Actions are triggered. Each rule has a specific state pattern it will check to determine what happens next. Both the object and the user of a SmartObject rule can have various states, which can be used in different SmartObject rules. In our case, we will need states for our mechanic and our objects to mark them as busy, broken, repaired, and so on. Once those states have been created, we can set up a state pattern. To create the states for our new rule, use the following:

1. In the Rule **Properties** window, find the **User** tab and click on **State Pattern**.

2. Click on the browse icon of the **State Pattern** property to open the state pattern selection window.

3. In the state pattern window, click on **New button**.

4. Enter `Broken` as the name for the new state and click on **OK**.

The State Pattern property of a SmartObject rule

This new **Broken** state is all we need for now. We will use it to determine whether our machines are broken or not. If you have a look at the state pattern window, you can see that there are **Busy** and **Idle** states already existing. Those states are always available by default and can be very useful when building new state patterns. We will utilize them in our state pattern later on to determine which object is *busy*.

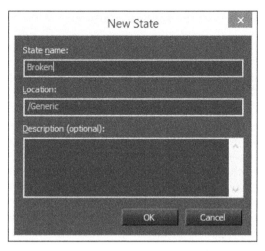

A new state called Broken is created to be used for our new rule

Now we have everything we need to start building our rule pattern. We have created new classes and new states we can use. All that is left now is to build a state pattern that does what we want and finally a SmartObject action, which will be executed once the pattern is matched.

Creating a SmartObject state pattern

The state pattern is the heart of a SmartObject rule. It determines what conditions have to be met for an action to be executed. A state pattern consists of certain states that have to be active, and others which cannot be active before the pattern starts an action.

User and Object

An environmental SmartObject rule has two main elements defining its behavior: **User** and **Object**. Both **User** and **Object** are usually regular CryENGINE entities that have been assigned a SmartObject class. When state patterns for a SmartObject rule are built, they are used to check for certain conditions for both **User** and **Object**. In our example, the mechanic AI would be **User** and the machines to be repaired would be **Object**. The Rule **Properties** window has special sections to set up the class and state patterns of **User** and **Object**.

Setting up the User and Object class

Before we set up the actual state pattern, we need to set up the classes of **User** and **Object** in the Rule **Properties** window:

1. In the Rule **Properties** window, find the **User** tab and click on the browse icon of the **Class** property to open the class selection window.

2. In the class selection window, click on the **MechanicGuy** class and then on **OK**.

This sets the class to **MechanicGuy** for the **User** class of our rule, the class we created earlier in this chapter. Now, let's set up the class for **Object**:

1. In the Rules **Properties** window, find the **Object** tab and click on the browse icon of the **Class** property to open the class selection window.

2. In the class selection window, click on the **Machine** class and then on **OK**.

Our **Object** has been assigned the **Machine** class. Both **User** and **Object** have a SmartObject class now. This means that only entities with the classes **Mechanic** and **Machine** will be taken into account when the rule is evaluated.

The state pattern

Now that we have the classes and state set up, let's have a look at the state pattern needed for our example: we want our mechanic AI to look around the world for broken objects and then go and repair them. What this means in terms of a state pattern is that an object's state should reflect whether it is broken or not. This is what the **Broken** state we created will be used for. The state pattern we are about to create could be rephrased like this: if there is a mechanic who is not busy in the range of a broken object, he should go and repair it.

Unfortunately, we cannot just type it in a script like this, but have to give it to the SmartObjects system in a different form. The state patterns for our example would look like the following:

* User state pattern: **NOT Busy**
* Objects state pattern: **Broken AND NOT Busy**

These states are set up in the SmartObject editor by including or excluding certain states to the pattern. In the state pattern selection window, you can click on each state to include or exclude it. Each click on a state switches its state. If you click on an included state, it will be excluded and vice versa. The state icon will change form an **X** to a checkbox, depending on its state. At the bottom of the window, you get an additional overview of what states are included and excluded.

To set up the state pattern for our *User*, perform the following steps:

1. In the Rule **Properties** window, find the **User** tab and click on the browse icon of the **State Pattern** property to open the state pattern selection window.

2. In the state pattern window, click on the **Busy** state until it is excluded.

3. Click on **OK** to close the state pattern window.

This will make sure the state pattern only takes **User** into account if he or she is not busy (the state **Busy** is excluded). Next, we have to set up the states for **Object**, which in our case are the machines to be repaired:

1. In the Rule **Properties** window, find the **Object** tab and click on the browse icon of the **State Pattern** property to open the state pattern selection window.

2. In the state pattern window, click on the **Busy** state until it is excluded.

3. In the state pattern window, click on the **Broken** state until it is included.

4. Click on **OK** to close the state pattern window.

This setup of the state pattern will make sure that the mechanic and the objects he is supposed to repair interact properly with each other. The **User** and **Object** sections of the Rule **Properties** window should now look like the following:

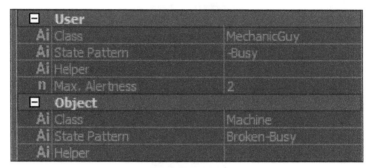

The final setup of the User and the Object of the SmartObject rule

The basic setup of the rule is now finished. The state pattern, as we defined it before, will make sure of the following: if a SmartObject with class **MechanicGuy** is *not* busy *and* a SmartObject with class **Machine** is broken but *not* busy, execute an action.

Creating an AIAction

We are almost done. Finally, we need to set up what is supposed to happen once our state pattern is matched. We can set this up in the **Action** section of the Rule **Properties** window. The two main things we need to set up here are the action which is to be executed and the state changes that are supposed to happen when the action starts and ends.

Selecting actions

There are different types of actions that can be executed once a state pattern is matched. For our example, we will use a simple AIAction that makes the user go to the object and *repair it*. To keep things simple, we will just have our mechanic walk to the broken object and switch it to a repaired state. Later on, we can of course extend the AIAction to play animations, particles effects, and so on.

Creating the action

To create a new action, simply open the flowgraph window and create a new AIAction:

1. In the flowgraph window, click on **File** and then on **New AI Action**.

2. Enter a name for the new action (for example, `RepairAction`) and save it in your game folder under `/Libs/ActionsGraphs/...`

Creating a new AIAction in the flow-graph

After the action has been created, it can be edited in the flowgraph window the same way as a regular flowgraph. There are a few things, however, where an AIAction is different from a regular flowgraph. Other than a normal entity-based flowgraph, an AIAction needs to have **AI:ActionStart** and **AI:ActionEnd** nodes, which start and end according to the corresponding action. The **AI:ActionStart** node has two EntityId outputs, which provide the graph with the EntityId of **User** and **Object** of the SmartObject rule. The **UserId** and **ObjectId** ports can also be used to trigger other nodes within the action. An AIAction will end, once the **AI:ActionEnd** node is triggered. The AIAction we require for our example should have **User** (our mechanic) walk to **Object** (a machine) and play a repair animation.

Simply use an **AI:Goto** node and an **Animations:PlayAnimation** node in your AIAction to have the AI walk to the object and play a repair animation. Make sure the **AI:Goto** node has a **StopDistance** of 1 m set up so our character stops a bit before actually reaching the object. In this example, the animation `relaxed_tac_idle_crouchrepairelectricbox_3p_01` has been used but it can be substituted with some particle effects and any other animation or even multiple animations played one after the other.

Also add a **DestroyableObject** node to the graph and use the **Object** EntityId for it. We are using the **Reset** port of the **DestroyableObject** to rest its state after it has been repaired. The following is how the AIAction should look:

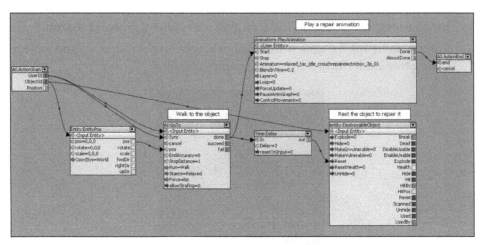

An AIAction that lets a character go to an object and play an animation

Make sure that the **AI:ActionStart** and **AI:ActionEnd** nodes are connected properly. If the **AI:ActionEnd** node is not triggered, the action will not end and block the AI from doing other things. After you are done setting up the action, make sure you save it. Unlike entity-based flowgraphs, AIActions are not automatically saved.

 AIActions always need to be saved manually and are not automatically saved when the CryENGINE level is saved.

Setting up the action and state changes

Now, we just need to set up our newly created action and make sure the **User** and **Object** states change properly when the action is started. This is done in the **Action** section of the Rule **Properties** window. The action section of the rule should look like what is shown in the following screenshot:

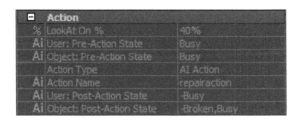

⊟	**Action**	
%	LookAt On %	40%
Ai	User: Pre-Action State	Busy
Ai	Object: Pre-Action State	Busy
	Action Type	AI Action
Ai	Action Name	repairaction
Ai	User: Post-Action State	-Busy
Ai	Object: Post-Action State	-Broken,Busy

Once all state patterns are matched, an action is executed. When this happens, you can additionally set up state changes that happen before and after the action is started as follows:

1. You can click on the **User**, **Object Pre-Action**, and **Post-Action** states to modify the states.

2. Set up the state patterns as shown in the preceding screenshot. The **Busy** state should be set for **User** and **Object** in the **Pre-Action** section. This will make sure that both objects are marked as **Busy** when the action starts to prevent this or other actions from triggering again.

3. In the **Post-Action** section, we remove the **Busy** state from both objects, which will make them available to perform further actions.

4. Additionally, we remove the **Broken** state from **Object** (our machine) to make it become *repaired*. Setting up the **Pre-Action** and **Post-Action** states is important and forgetting to set them up might lead to actions not being triggered at all or even being triggered multiple times.

 Setting up **Pre-Action** and **Post-Action** states is an important part of the SmartObject rule creation. It will ensure actions are not triggered multiple times.

The setup of our SmartObject rule is complete now. We can now go ahead and start using it in our levels. In our example level, we will now need to assign our entities the right SmartObject classes and make sure any flowgraph scripting we might need is set up.

Getting the level ready

Let's start by assigning the correct classes to the entities placed in our level. Currently, there is not too much going on in our level. We placed one AI character and a couple of barrels.

1. Start by selecting the AI character and assign him a SmartObject class. In the Properties section of the AI character, set the **SmartObjectClass** parameter to **MechanicGuy**. This will make the AI character our mechanic.

2. Next, in the Properties section of the DestroyableObjects we placed, set the **SmartObjectClass** parameter to **Machine**. This will make the DestroyableObjects we placed act as machines that can be repaired.

3. Finally, we need to make sure that the **DestroyableObject** gets *broken*. For our example, we will trigger the **Broken** state to be set when the object is damaged. This way we can just shoot directly at the entity to break it quickly. Create a simple flowgraph which looks like the following:

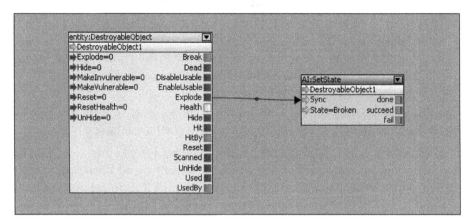

We are using the **AI:SetState** node to add the state **Broken** to the entity once the **Explode** output triggers. Simply type `Broken` into the State property of the node. You can set up as many DestroyableObjects as you like this way. As long as their state is properly changed, they will trigger the SmartObject rule. Now, every time one of our barrels in the level is shot, its state will change and trigger the SmartObject action.

Testing the SmartObject rule

Now that all the setup is done, let's test our work. Jump into the game and shoot one of the barrels. Once the barrel is broken, its state will change and you will see our AI walking towards the barrel to *repair it*.

You can go ahead now and add more DestroyableObjects and AI characters to your level or modify the AIAction further. As long as the SmartObject classes are set up properly, you can have dozens of AI repairing dozens of machines at the same time.

Troubleshooting

Since creating new SmartObject rules is a rather complex process, a few mistakes can happen along the way. The following is a short troubleshooting list, just in case the SmartObject example does not work right away:

- **The AI character does not move**: Check if the AI navigation has been set up properly. An AI not moving is most likely always caused by an incorrect navigation setup. Also check if the AI character is close enough to the things he is supposed to repair. In the properties of a rule, the maximum distance for the rule to become active can be set. If the character is not moving, try to change the **DistanceFrom** and **DistanceTo** parameters in the **Limits** section of the properties of the rule.

- **Destroying a DestroyableObject does not trigger the action**: Check the rule setup to see if all the states are set up correctly. Also, check if all objects have the correct SmartObject classes assigned.

- **The AIAction only works once**: Check if the Pre-Action and Post-Action states have been set up correctly. When the Post-Action states are not set correctly, the action might not be triggered a second time.

- **The AIAction does not work or does not do what it should**: Check if AIAction has been built correctly, using the right **EntityIds** and the **AI:ActionEnd** node is triggered.

Debugging SmartObjects

There are a few very useful console commands that will help you debug SmartObject behaviors. When working with SmartObjects and testing your rules, it is recommended to turn on the following debug modes:

```
ai_DebugDraw 1
ai_DrawSmartObjects 1
```

This will display useful information about SmartObject classes and states on the screen, which will help you find out what's happening. SmartObject states and classes are displayed on top of the entity and let you see exactly what is happening. More information on the various AI debug draw commands can be found in the official CryENGINE documentation at `http://docs.cryengine.com/display/SDKDOC2/AI+Debug+Draw`. Utilizing the AI debug draw commands can help you to track down AI issues and problems faster and more efficiently.

Debugging AIActions

AIActions can be debugged the same way as regular flowgraphs using the visual flowgraph debugging tools. Most problems with AIActions, however, are related to the **User** or **Object** EntityIds not set properly. The following screenshot shows SmartObject states displayed on top of the entities in CryENGINE:

Changing states from Lua

In our example, we used a simple flowgraph to change the SmartObject state of our entity when it breaks. This works, but is not very flexible since we need to do extra flowgraph work for every additional DestroyableObject we place. To make things a bit easier for us, we can also modify the entity script to switch the state automatically whenever the entity is destroyed. To do this, simply add the following line to the Explode() function of the DestroyableObject script:

```
AI.ModifySmartObjectStates( self.id, "Broken" );
```

This will add the Broken state to the entity every time it gets destroyed.

Summary

In this chapter, we learned all about the SmartObject system and how to use it to create more interactive game environments. We had a look at the SmartObjects editor and learned how to use it to create new rules, classes, and actions. We built a simple example of a mechanic reacting to things in a level, breaking and then repairing them. The SmartObject system can be used for many more complex things, which will help make your game more immersive. And of course, the use of the SmartObject system is not limited to AI entities, but can be used with player characters as well. The same rules built for AI entities will also apply to other entities as long as the SmartObject states are set up for the corresponding entities. The great thing about the SmartObject system and the way it works is that it's quite easy to use, even for non-programmers. In our example, in this chapter, we have built an AI behavior without really touching code or writing any complicated behavior scripts.

In the next chapter, things will get a bit more visual and we will look at all the eye candy CryENGINE has to offer. The engine is packed with shaders and effects that allow you to create breathtaking scenarios. We will have a look at a lot of those effects and use them to improve the visuals of our game.

Eye Candy – Particles, Lens Flares, and More

You have probably heard this before: "Gameplay is more important than graphics". This rather old saying is still true today when it comes to game production. However, this does not mean that good visuals are not important. Good rendering quality and high visual fidelity go a long way when you are trying to get the player immersed in your game. CryENGINE excels when it comes to rendering beautiful and realistic environments. As a developer, CryENGINE offers you a vast array of shaders, effects, and tools, which all help you create stunningly beautiful environments for your game. This is where CryENGINE really stands out from the crowd of real-time 3D engines.

Most of CryENGINE's rendering and postprocessing effects can be controlled and set up from Sandbox. In this chapter, we will take a look at what types of effects CryENGINE has to offer and how best to use them in a project. We will look at the different ways to use and set up this extra bit of eye candy that will help your game look a bit shinier.

Types of eye candy

Eye candy can be added to CryENGINE in many different places. You can improve the visuals of your game by using different shaders on your materials, adding postprocessing effects, or putting more particles into the scene. The usual ways to improve the looks of your game are:

- Adding situational postprocessing effects
- Using more complex materials for objects
- Adding more particle effects
- Tweaking the time of day settings

In this chapter, we will look at some of the most common ways to improve the visual fidelity of your level and how to use them.

Particle effects

CryENGINE ships with an extremely powerful and flexible particle system. The integrated particle editor allows you to create new particle effects and review and tweak them in real time. Not only is the particle system in CryENGINE easy to use, it also provides you with state-of-the-art rendering features, such as soft particles, particle shadows, and realistic particle lighting.

Working with particle effects in CryENGINE

Particle effects in CryENGINE are basically normal entities and can also be used as such. They can be added to flowgraphs, customized with Lua scripts, and be linked and spawned like regular entities. The actual particle emitter and its settings are stored inside an XML data structure, which is referenced by the entity. The behavior and visuals of the particle emitter are set up and customized using the CryENGINE particle editor, which is a part of the Sandbox toolkit. The usual workflow to create particle effects in CryENGINE looks like this:

1. Create and organize a new particle library.
2. Create particle textures and materials.
3. Set up particle properties and parameters.

The workflow itself is quick and simple. Most of your time, however, is spent in step three when the particle has to be set up and tweaked. High quality particle effects can sometimes require hours of polishing and tweaking. Although CryENGINE's particle rendering system is extremely powerful and provides you with features like *soft particles* and *shadow casting particles*, the most important aspect is proper setup and tweaking of the particle parameters.

The particle editor

The CryENGINE particle editor is an extremely complex and sophisticated tool, which allows you to create stunning and realistic particle effects. Effects are created by customizing particle emitters and saving them in a particle library. The particle editor is part of the **DatabaseView** window and its layout is similar to the **Archetype**, **Prefab**, and **GameToken** libraries.

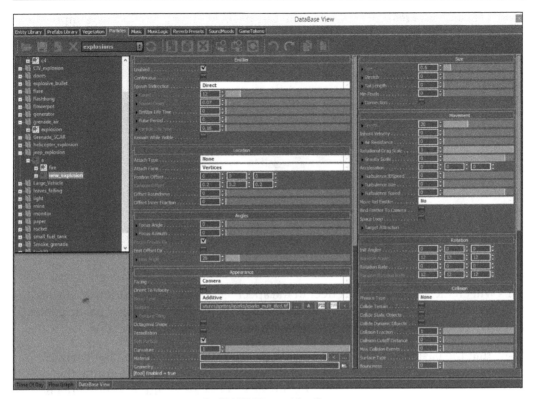

CryENGINE's particle editor

Although the particle editor might look quite overwhelming at first, it is really not complicated to use. Just like with most other tools in the **Database View**, the main controls to create, edit, and delete libraries can be found at the top of the window. The left side of the editor window is taken up by a list of all the particle effects in the current library and a preview window of the currently selected particle effect.

Creating a new particle effect

A new particle effect can either be placed in a new particle library or one that already exists. For the example we are about to see, let's create a new particle library. Open the particle editor inside the **Database View** window and add a new particle library using the **Add Library** button.

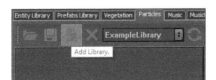

Creating a new particle library in the particle editor

Now we can start creating new effects in our particle library. To do this, simply click on the **Add New Item** button in the menu bar and enter a group and effect name into the dialog box.

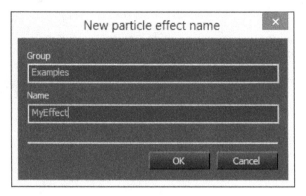

Particle effects are organized in groups

This will create a new particle effect in the specified group. This workflow allows you to nest particle effects and organize them more efficiently. Larger particle effects are often organized in multiple groups with many subeffects in each one.

Now that the basic effect has been created, we can start customizing the particle effect. The particle editor has dozens of different settings which determine the visuals of a particle effect as well as its physical behavior, lighting, sound effects, and so on. Although all of those properties are documented in the official CryENGINE documentation, working with the particle editor can be a bit overwhelming at first.

The official CryENGINE documentation provides a great amount of in-depth information about each parameter in the particle editor. Be sure to use it as a reference when modifying parameters.

Despite the large amount of available options, creating a new particle effect is not really difficult at all. In the following example, we will create a fire effect. The particle editor, of course, allows you to create much more sophisticated effects than just fire, but it is a good point to start.

Customizing the particle parameters

We have already created a new particle effect and now just need to adjust its parameters to make it look the way we want. The element which determines the quality of the particle effect the most is the texture being used. Having high quality textures will go a long way in creating believable particle effects. Let us start by picking a fire texture and setting it in the properties of the particle effect. Luckily, the CryENGINE SDK already ships with some great example textures we can use for our example. For our fire example, let us use one of those textures:

1. Select the texture `../GameSDK/Textures/sprites/fire/fireball_anim_b.dds` in the **Appearance** section of the particle effect parameters.

2. Select the **Additive** setting in the **Blend Type** drop-down list to make sure the particle is rendered properly.

3. The animated texture contains an 8 x 8 grid of textures. Set the **Tiles X** and **Tiles Y** parameters to **8**.

4. Set the **Anim Frames Count** to **64** (8 x 8 sprites inside the texture).

5. Set **Anim Cycle** to **Loop** to make the fire animation loop properly.

6. Check the **Anim Blend** checkbox to blend the sprites smoothly.

7. Check the **Soft Particle** checkbox to make sure there is no ugly clipping with the terrain or other objects.

The **Anim Framerate** property will be controlled by the particles' life if it is set to **0**. For example, if the lifetime of the particle is set to 1 second, then the whole sheet will be played in 1 second even if the sheet has 30, 64, or 100 frames in it. If a value on **Anim Framerate** is set, then the set will play according to that number per second. If the particle effect has, for example, 64 frames in its texture with a lifetime of 1 second and **Anim Framerate** set to 30, it means the emitter will only play 30 frames from the sheet.

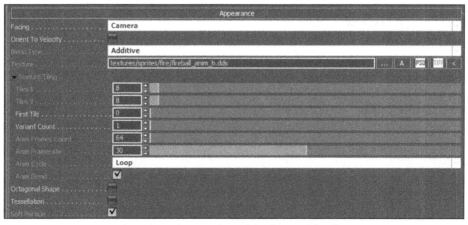

An animated texture is used for this particle effect

With the preceding steps, we have created the first basic particle effect. In order to get a higher quality effect, we are using an animated texture, which contains multiple tiles. We have set the tiling to a grid of 8 x 8 to match the individual images contained inside the texture. Things do not look too impressive, however, since we have not set up any movement parameters yet. When you drag the particle effect into your level, you will not see anything right away. Let's try and set up the rest of the parameters so we can preview our particle effect.

Remember that you can just drag-and-drop particle effects from the particle editor directly into your level to preview them in your level environment. Hitting the **ReloadScripts** button in the **RollupBar** will reload the particle effect and restart noncontinuous effects.

Next, we have to define how many particles our emitter should have and how long they will be *alive*. This can be set up in the **Emitter** section of the particle:

1. In the **Emitter** section, set the **Count** parameter to 20.
2. Set the **Particle Life Time** to 2.

When you look at your particle effect now, you can see a lot of flames spawning, all in one area. Since the behavior of a real-life fire is very chaotic by nature, we should add a bit of movement and rotation to the effect in **Movement**. First, let us add a bit of randomness:

1. In the **Location** section, set the **Random Offset** option to 0.2, 0.2, and 0.1.
2. In the **Movement** section, set the **Speed** option to 0.5.

Now, we have a decent flame effect moving somewhat realistically.

Tweaking the effect

Now that we have a working base effect, we can tweak and polish all kinds of things to make it look better. We can add light sources, sound effects, materials, or physical properties. For an effect like fire, we would now add subeffects, such as ember and smoke, and tweak those until they look good. However, the number of customization options is so huge that a single book could be filled just with discussing the particle editor, particles, and how to customize them. Instead of focusing on the plethora of customization options in the particle editor, we will rather look at different ways to improve the visuals of our game by using CryENGINE's particle system.

Particle effects at runtime

After a particle has been created in the particle editor, you can place them as entities in your level. Although you cannot change all of the effect's parameters at runtime, you have access to certain options which let you modify the behavior of the effect, such as:

- Size
- Movement
- Speed
- Count

This allows you to use gameplay data and feed it to the particle effect in real time. You can place particle effects in your level and dynamically adjust them depending on what is happening in your game. You can either directly change the properties of the entity in a script or simply adjust particle behavior in a flowgraph.

Have a look at this simple flowgraph:

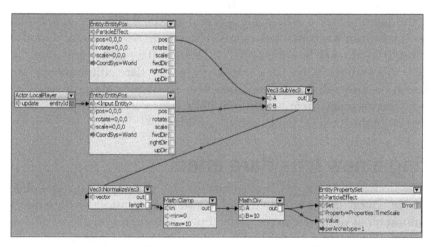

A simple flowgraph slowing down a particle effect

The preceding screenshot shows a simple flowgraph which measures the distance between the player and a particle effect. It then clamps the distance down to 10m and scales it to a value between 0 and 1. By using this flowgraph, the closer you get to the particle effect, the more it will slow down, creating a cool local slow-motion effect. Working with particles this way allows you to create all kinds of great effects, taking into account what is currently happening in your level. More information on the individual parameters of a particle effect can be found in the official CryENGINE documentation at `http://docs.cryengine.com/display/SDKDOC2/Particle+Editor+Params`.

Lens flares

One of the newest additions to the list of CryENGINE rendering capabilities is the lens flare system. The lens flare system, which was added to CryENGINE only recently, is more than just a simple lens flare effect. It is a full-blown system with tools to create and set up new lens flares easily. In real life, lens flare effects are caused by light sources hitting a lens and the light being scattered.

Of course, the approach that CryENGINE takes is a bit simpler and does not simulate actual rays of light being scattered on the game camera. In the engine, lens flare effects are caused by lights and can be seen as a property of light sources. You can have any light source in CryENGINE cause lens flare effects by adding a lens flare property to it. This workflow makes it very easy to add lens flares to your level. Once a light has a lens flare property set, a special lens flare material will be applied, which allows rendering of all kinds of effects.

The lens flare editor

Just like many other CryENGINE systems, the lens flare editor is integrated into Sandbox and intended for use by designers and artists. It allows you to build custom lens flare effects from basic effect elements. There is no need to go and modify scripts or XML files to create new lens flare effects. The lens flare editor will allow you to create them in Sandbox easily. The controls of the lens flare editor are similar to those of the other tools integrated into DatabaseView. You can create, edit, and delete lens flare effects and organize them in different library files. By default, all flare library files are saved in the `Game/Libs/Flares/..` folder.

Creating a new lens flare effect

The CryENGINE SDK is shipped with a neat library of sample lens flare effects at your disposal. These effects will do the job if you want to add lens flare effects to the most common types of light sources. Sometimes, however, it might be necessary to create custom effects. The lens flare editor offers you a set of basic effects which you can combine in many ways to create new effects.

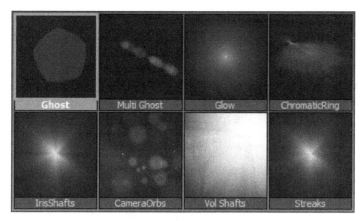

A lens flare effect is built from basic elements

A set of eight basic elements is provided with the editor. Any number of these elements can be used in your flare effects to get the desired look. To create a new lens flare effect using the basic flare elements, follow these steps:

1. Open the lens flare editor and create a new lens flare library.

2. Click on **Add New Item** to create a new effect in your library.

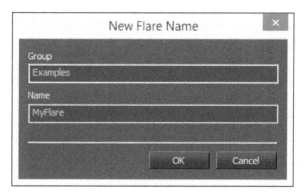

A new lens flare effect is created

3. Drag-and-drop any of the **CameraOrbs** effects from the **Basic Set** window onto your newly created element in the **Element Tree** window.

You now have a new lens flare effect in your library. If it is selected and you look at the **Element Tree** window, you can see the composition of the effect. Currently, your effect only has one subeffect called *orbs*. Before we go ahead and add more subeffects, let's customize the effect a bit so we can preview it. The preview window in the center of the lens flare editor will not display anything yet since we have not selected the correct textures to be used for this effect. Let's customize our effect so that we can preview it properly as follows:

1. Select the effect root in the **Element Tree** window.
2. Set the **Distance Fading factor** parameter to `0.1`.
3. Set the **Brightness** parameter to `4`.
4. Select the **orbs** subeffect in the **Element Tree** window.
5. Set the **Orb Texture** parameter to `GameSDK/Textures/lights/lens_flares/circular_bokeh_blurry.dds`.
6. Set the **Lens Texture** parameter to `../GameSDK/Textures/lights/lens_flares/visor_scratch.dds`.
7. Check the **Enable lens texture** checkbox.

Now you can preview the lens flare effect in the **Preview** window of the lens flare editor. You can move the camera around in the **Preview** window by pressing the middle mouse button and moving the mouse. The right mouse button will reset your camera position if you navigate out of the view of the effect.

 You can navigate inside the lens flare preview window by pressing the middle mouse button and moving the mouse. The right mouse button will reset your view.

Assigning a lens flare effect to a light

Now that the lens flare effect has been created, you can either keep on improving it by tweaking the settings and adding more subeffects or you can assign it to a light source and use it in your level. Assigning your lens flare effect to a light source is simple. Just drag-and-drop the flare effect from the lens flare editor onto a *Light* entity in Sandbox's perspective view. When you drop the effect on a light entity, it will be applied to the light and the lens flare property of the light will be set. Once you have your effect applied to a light source in your level, you can keep on tweaking it. Just as with CryENGINE's particle system, the number of options and parameters is too large to be covered in this book. Have a look at the official CryENGINE documentation to get more information about the specific parameters of each flare effect.

Lens flare effects caused by the sun

One of the most common light sources used in CryENGINE levels is the sun, which is set up in the time of day editor. Since the sun in CryENGINE is not a light entity but rather a complex creation set up in the time of day editor, you cannot drag-and-drop a flare effect onto it. Adding a lens flare effect to the sun is extremely easy. Simply place a light source in your level and make sure the **AttachToSun** checkbox is checked. This will cause this light entity to render its lens flare effect on top of the sun instead of on itself.

Postprocessing effects and the flow graph

Many of the postprocessing effects available in the engine can easily be controlled from the flowgraph. Although it does not always give you full control of every aspect of each effect, using the flowgraph to trigger a certain postprocessing effect is one of the easiest and quickest ways when working with postprocessing effects in the engine. The flowgraph provides you with a lot of useful nodes that allow you to quickly access all kinds of effects. Most of those nodes can be found in the Image folder of the component nodes.

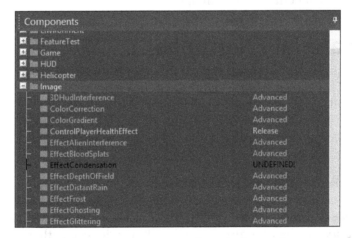

The Image component nodes in the flowgraph

Using most of these nodes is quite easy and straightforward. The **Image:FilterBlur** node, for example, is rather simple and can be used to put a simple blur effect on the screen. The amount of blur could be hardcoded in the flowgraph node or even provided dynamically. For example, this would allow you to fade in the blur effect depending on the distance or state of different objects.

This is an example of a simple flowgraph which shows how to fade in a blur effect once a trigger is entered:

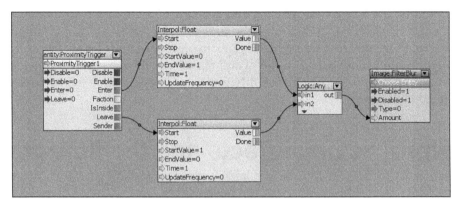

A simple flowgraph fading in a blur postprocessing effect

These kind of constructions can be used in regular flowgraphs, flowgraph modules, and AIAction graphs. It is a common technique to set up local areas in a level with an image effect, such as color correction or a special filter. Usually, these effects are then triggered by the player entering the area.

Using material FX graphs

Material effect graphs are a special type of flowgraph triggered by the material effects system. This allows you to easily trigger flowgraphs when something in the game world is hit. There is no need to write any code or script; you can just let the material effects system take care of it for you. Have a look at the graphs in the /MaterialFX folder in the flowgraph editor window to get an idea of how material effects graphs are set up.

If you have worked with the material effects system before, you might know that most of the configuration takes place in the XML files located in the /Libs/ MaterialEffects/ folder. These configuration files contain the XML tables that define what happens when certain materials collide with each other.

For each material effect defined within the material effects system, you can also define an effects flowgraph to be executed, which takes into account the distance to the player position, intensity, and other parameters. This allows you to use all of the image effect nodes within a flowgraph, which is triggered by something like a bullet hit.

Creating a custom material FX graph

A new material effects graph can be created easily by adding a new file in the `/Libs/MaterialEffects/FXLibs/` folder as follows:

1. Create a new XML file inside the `/Libs/MaterialEffects/FXLibs/` folder. You can name the file anything you want. The name of the XML file is not important for the functionality.

2. Create a simple XML structure within the file which defines the material effects graph:

```
<FXLib>
  <Effect name="my_matfx" delay="0.05">
    <FlowGraph name="my_matfx_graph" maxdist="20"/>
  </Effect>
</FXLib>
```

Before moving on to the next step, let's have a look at the XML structure. The new file we created only contains one effect, which is called `my_matfx`.

The only component in this effect is a `FlowGraph` entry.

```
<FlowGraph name="my_matfx_graph" maxdist="20"/>
```

The preceding line will execute the flowgraph `my_matfx_graph` when the player is no further than 20m. Of course, there are many more components that can be added to the material effect, such as sound, particles, and decals. But for this example, we will focus on executing a flowgraph, since it provides us with the possibility to apply all kinds of postprocessing effects when triggered.

Now that the material effect has been created, we need to add it to the material effects library. The library `../Libs/MaterialEffects/MaterialEffects.xml` contains definitions of the events that can occur between different materials and their surface types, such as a bullet hitting a piece of wood.

		mat_metal	mat_metal_nofric
mat_invulnerable	mat_invulnerable	bulletimpacts:blank_event	bulletimpacts:blank_event
PistolBullet	PistolBullet	bulletimpacts:hit_mat_metal	bulletimpacts:hit_mat_metal
RifleBullet	RifleBullet	my_mat_fx:my_matfx	bulletimpacts:hit_mat_metal
tank125	tank125	bulletimpacts:grenade_hit_mat_default	bulletimpacts:grenade_hit_mat_de
MGbullet	MGbullet	bulletimpacts:hit_mat_metal	bulletimpacts:hit_mat_metal
melee	melee	bulletimpacts:melee_hit_mat_metal	bulletimpacts:melee_hit_mat_met
tornado	tornado	tornado:generic	tornado:generic
explosivegrenade	explosivegrenade	collisions:grenade_default	collisions:grenade_default
explosivegrenade_explode	explosivegrenade_explode	bulletimpacts:grenade_hit_mat_default	bulletimpacts:grenade_hit_mat_de
explosivegrenade_explode_underwater	explosivegrenade_explode_underwater	bulletimpacts:grenade_hit_mat_water	bulletimpacts:grenade_hit_mat_w
footstep_player	footstep_player	footstep_player:metal_thick	footstep_player:metal_thick
footstep_grunt	footstep_grunt	footstep_grunt:metal_thick	footstep_grunt:metal_thick
footstep	footstep	footstep_grunt:metal_thick	footstep_grunt:metal_thick
bodyfall	bodyfall	foley:bf_metal_thick	foley:bf_metal_thick
vfx_Abrams	vfx_Abrams	vehicles:heavy_metal	vehicles:heavy_metal
vfx_HMMWV	vfx_HMMWV	vehicles:light_metal	vehicles:light_metal
vfx_Helicopter	vfx_Helicopter	vehicles:helicopter_metal	vehicles:helicopter_metal

The material effects library defines events between materials

It is recommended that you use MS Excel to edit the material effects library file. It is possible to use a text editor, but considering the complexity of the file, Excel is a better alternative. Within the library, events are organized in rows and columns. You can choose where to enter your new effect depending on what materials you want to trigger your effect with. For our example, we will just overwrite an existing event and change it so that it plays our newly created material effect:

1. Find the cell located in the row labeled `RifleBullet` and the column labeled `mat_metal`.

2. Enter `my_mat_fx:my_matfx` into the corresponding cell.

This will tell the engine to play the material effect `my_matfx` located in the `my_mat_fx` library whenever there is an event, such as a collision occurring between the surface types `RifleBullet` and `mat_metal`. Basically, when you now shoot a metal surface with a rifle, your custom material effect will be triggered and its flowgraph executed. The last thing to do before the effect will work properly would be to create the effects flowgraph, which we defined in our effect. Let's have a look at our effect again:

```
<Effect name="my_matfx" delay="0.05">
  <FlowGraph name="my_matfx_graph" maxdist="20"/>
</Effect>
```

As you can see, our effect sets the flowgraph `my_matfx_graph` to be executed. We now need to create this flowgraph as follows:

1. Open the flowgraph editor, click on **File**, and then on **New MaterialFX Graph**.

2. Enter `my_matfx_graph` as a name for the new graph and save it in the `../Libs/MaterialEffects/Flowgraphs/` folder.

3. Create a simple flowgraph triggering a visual effect and save it.

The flowgraph you create for this effect can be as simple or complex as you like. Two nodes which should always be present, however, should be the **MaterialFX:HUDStartFX** and **MaterialFX:HUDEndFX** nodes. These nodes make sure that the action gets executed and terminated properly. This is what a simple example material effects graph should look like:

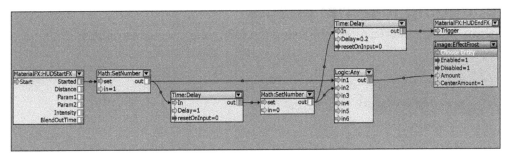

A simple material effects graph triggering a frost effect

This simple flowgraph triggers a fullscreen frost effect whenever it is being executed. The names of the material effects flowgraph nodes (**HUDStartFX** and **HUDEndFX**) suggest that only **head-up display** (**HUD**) effects can be triggered in these types of flowgraphs. You can, however, trigger any kind of action you like. Nothing is stopping you from building a material effects flowgraph that throws the player into the air, spawns AI enemies, or interacts with GameTokens. Although the primary use of material effect graphs is to display postprocessing effects, it is up to you as to what extent you want to use the system.

Testing the new material effect

To test this new effect, simply shoot a metal surface with a standard rifle. Every time a hit is detected, your flowgraph will be triggered. Keep in mind that if you have made changes to the material effects libraries and created new flowgraphs, you might need to restart Sandbox in order to properly test the new effect. Smaller changes in the material effects library can also simply be reloaded using the `mfx_reload` console variable.

 You can use the `mfx_Reload` and `mfx_ReloadFGEffects` console commands to reload the material effect files without restarting Sandbox.

Debugging material effects

You can debug material effects by using the following console variables:

- `mfx_Debug`
- `mfx_DebugFlowGraphFX`
- `mfx_DebugVisual`
- `mfx_DebugVisualFilter`
- `mfx_Debug`

This set of variables allows you to visually display and filter all effects going on in the scene. The `mfx_DebugVisual` console variable is especially useful since it will draw information about the material effects and the event that caused it to be drawn into the 3D scene.

Postprocessing in TrackView

The **TrackView** tool in CryENGINE is a fantastic tool to build cutscenes and movie-like sequences. Effects like motion blur, depth of field, and other postprocessing effects can easily be controlled from TrackView. Triggering postprocessing effects from within TrackView can be done in multiple ways. You can do either of the following:

- Create individual effect tracks within the sequence
- Use track events to trigger effects in a flow graph

These are the two most common ways to work with postprocessing effects in your sequences.

Using effect tracks in a TrackView sequence

TrackView allows you to add various effect tracks directly into your sequence. To do this, simply right-click on the **Director** node of a TrackView sequence. The context menu will show you a list of all the tracks available for addition as shown in the following screenshot:

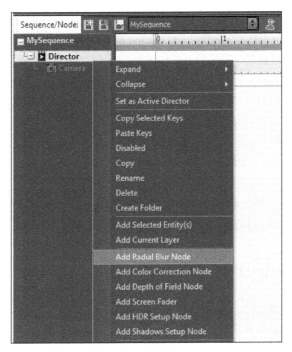

Effect tracks can be added to any sequence

You can add tracks for basic effects, such as depth of field or blur, directly to the sequence or use a script or console variable to call them. Controlling postprocessing effects this way gives you full control over the behavior and visuals of the selected effect.

The curve editor of TrackView, for example, allows you to smoothly blend effects.

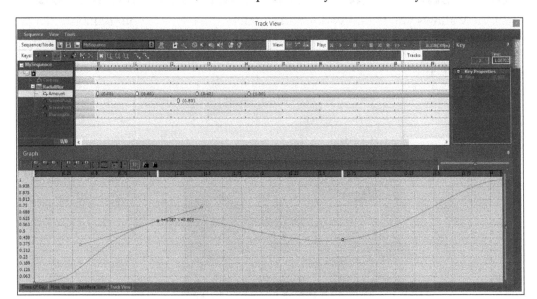

The curve editor provides full control over a postprocessing effect in a sequence

Using track events

Track events allow you to trigger a flowgraph from any point in your sequence. In this way, you can have complex flowgraphs provide the effects for your sequence. To create a new track event, follow these steps:

1. Right-click on the **Director** node of your sequence and select **Add Event** from the context menu.

2. Enter a name for the new event track and click on **OK**.

3. Right-click on the **Director** node of your sequence and select **Edit Events** from the context menu.

4. In the event menu, click on **Add**, enter a name for the event, click on **OK**, and close the event menu.

5. Double-click anywhere in the newly created event track to create a new event key.

6. In the properties of the created key, select the event you just created from the event drop-down list.

Now when you play your sequence and the timeline reaches the event key, the event will be triggered. To react to this event in your flowgraphs, you need to add a track event node. In your flowgraph, simply open the context menu and select **Add Track Event**. This will add a track event node, which allows you to select a sequence and react to all events it has set up.

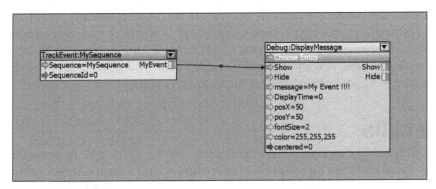

The TrackEvent node outputs all sequence events

Now, whenever the event key is reached in the sequence, the **TrackEvent** node will trigger an output, which can be used to trigger all kinds of effects in turn.

Performance considerations

With many great effects and shaders at your disposal, one of the biggest risks is overloading a scene with too many effects and slowing down the frame rate in the process. Most shaders and effects in CryENGINE are fast and optimized. These can be used without much performance impact. However, when too many effects are used in a scene, the frame rate might be impacted considerably. During game development, often so-called *beautification passes* are done to a level or environment. During those passes, a lot of eye candy and polish is added. It is important that during those beautification tasks, the performance and frame rate are closely monitored to catch any performance impacts early on.

Luckily, CryENGINE provides a powerful set of profiling tools that will help you identify performance bottlenecks easily.

Overdraw

The term **Overdraw** is commonly used in performance profiling to determine how expensive each pixel in a scene is. Transparent materials and postprocessing effects cause a high number of pixel shader instructions per pixel and can make the rendering of a pixel on the screen very expensive. Especially when a lot of large particles are used, overdraw in a scene can increase drastically. When other postprocessing effects are going on in addition to many particle activities, the performance can be seriously impacted. When working with particles and postprocessing effects, you should make regular use of the r_MeasureOverdraw console variable to get an overview of the overdraw situation of your scene.

Draw calls

A draw call is made every time the engine instructs the GPU to draw something on the scene. Draw calls can be caused by many things, and a high number of draw calls can impact performance considerably. A high number of rendering materials is the most common reason for a high number of draw calls in a CryENGINE environment. Other things such as postprocessing can also increase the number of draw calls, but mainly a high number of materials and submaterials will affect the number of draw calls. The number of draw calls that is acceptable for you depends on the hardware of your target platform. If you are developing a game for Xbox 360, you would aim for a draw call number of 1,500 - 2,000, while for a game targeted at a high-end PC, you could easily go beyond that and have 3,000 draw calls in a scene. During development, it is important to keep the number of draw calls in mind. CryENGINE offers you great tools to monitor the number of draw calls. You can use the console variable r_stats to get an overview of the current draw call situation.

Summary

In this chapter, we had a look at some of the eye candy CryENGINE has to offer. We learned about how we can add particle effects and lens flares to our game using the built-in editors and tools. We also took a quick look at some of the performance problems that can arise when too many effects are being used in a scene.

In the next and final chapter of this book, we will discuss the challenges you will face when you are finally ready to ship your game. We will focus on getting your CryENGINE game ready to ship to stores and digital distribution platforms.

10
Shipping the Build

One of the most exciting moments of your game production process will be the time when everything is finished and you are getting ready to ship your build. Depending on the size of your project, this task can be quick and easy or time consuming.

In this chapter, we will take a look at the important tasks involved in getting your game ready at the hands of players. Each game engine has a different pipeline and different requirements when it comes to packing up a shippable build. We will look at the best practices and common tasks related to this final step in the game production pipeline.

Getting your game ready to ship

When is your game ready to ship? Well, *when it is done* you might answer. Obviously, your game will be released once it is finished and all the features are implemented. However, there are a few things you should consider before you declare your CryENGINE game ready for release.

Once your game is released and people are playing it, first impressions are created. It doesn't matter if it is a AAA game or a free mod for an already existing game. You can always patch and improve your game later, but once players dislike your game based on their first impression, it becomes very difficult to get them to change their minds again. This is why you should aim at releasing your game in the best possible state, as polished and free of bugs as possible.

This chapter will provide you with a lot of useful hints and best practices that will help you avoid the usual pitfalls, such as performance problems, shipping unnecessary files, or worst of all, shipping a broken game.

Optimizing performance

Depending on your target platform, performance problems in your CryENGINE game will be more or less a critical issue. In general, developing for older hardware, such as the Xbox 360 or PlayStation 3 proves to be more challenging due to the limited memory and other limiting hardware factors of that console generation.

The bad news here is that performance problems are rarely something you fix quickly at the end of the production cycle. Maintaining a good frame rate throughout your development is an ongoing effort. The usual last-minute fixes may include:

- Removing error and log spam
- Reducing texture and polygon count
- Adding LODs to your 3D models

Unfortunately, there won't be enough time to go back and change or optimize models. While reducing the texture size on certain objects might be feasible with a minimum effort, creating new LODs or models takes significantly more time. You can increase performance slightly by removing specular and normal maps from materials where these are not really needed. But do not do so without testing, since removing these can make a big difference in different lighting conditions. As materials are sometimes shared, this can have unexpected side effects.

To avoid those troubles at the end of a project, make sure you always work within the budget appropriate for your target platform.

Optimizing levels

The most common way to gain a significant increase in frame rate without investing a large amount of time is to tweak the parameters and console variables of individual CryENGINE levels and environments.

Level configuration files

The CryENGINE configuration filesystem is quite sophisticated and allows you to create individual configuration files per level. What this means is that you can create a `level.cfg` configuration file and place it inside the corresponding level folder. A regular CryENGINE build always has the `system.cfg` configuration file located in the root of the CryENGINE folder. This file has all the game specific configuration setups. Since the levels of your game can be quite different from each other in both size and scope, it makes sense to create level-specific configuration files. Is one of your levels really heavy on vegetation objects? No problem, just add a level-specific configuration file, which has the console variables set a bit more aggressively. Does one of your levels have an unusually high view distance? Just set up the object LODs to be switched a bit sooner and gain an instant increase in performance.

 To create a new level-specific configuration file, simply create a new empty text file inside the level's folder and rename it to `level.cfg`.

The console variables put into this level-specific file will be applied when the level is loaded, after the console variables from the `system.cfg` file have already been applied. In this way, each level can have customized settings for things such as vegetation, shadows, or LODs.

Optimizing shadows

CryENGINE really excels when it comes to great-looking real-time shadows. Not only do shadows in CryENGINE look good and smooth, but they are also customizable in a great amount of detail. A large number of shadows, or rather shadow casting objects and light sources, can significantly impact performance and increase the number of shadow-related draw calls.

Although real-time shadows look great and help improve the visuals of your game, it is not always necessary to have every object in a level cast a shadow. A common mistake is to have too many objects and lights cast a shadow. What professional teams do very often as part of their performance improvement efforts is a so-called *shadow pass*.

In this shadow optimization pass, a designer or artist goes over all the objects in a level and disables the shadow casting settings for all lights and objects in the level. This includes turning off shadows for decals. After this, the level will look significantly worse than before but with an improved frame rate.

In the next step, the designer goes over all assets and turns on the shadow casting options *where it makes sense*, meaning where it makes a *visual* difference. This usually leads to a greatly reduced number of shadow-related draw calls, compared to the original level. The reason for this is that during the construction and design of a level environment, level designers do not always have the time to pay attention to tweaking shadow options properly. A shadow pass done at the end of the production usually improves the frame rate a lot without lowering the quality of the visuals significantly.

Almost no difference: The left image has all object shadows enabled, while the right one has all shadows disabled

In addition to just turning object shadows on or off, there is a plethora of options that allow you to set up lights to cast shadows only under certain circumstances. Each light source, for example, has the option to only cast shadows when the game is running in a certain setting. This allows you to set up things like additional lights that only cast shadows on the **High** or **VeryHigh** quality setting.

Furthermore, each light source can be customized in a great amount of detail with respect to the shadow quality and update rate. All of these tweaks and optimizations can be done directly in the properties of the entity.

The properties of a light entity allow for a lot of customization to improve performance

Vegetation

When it comes to profiling level performance, the vegetation setup ends up being one of the most expensive things in a level. While they look great, a high number of vegetation objects in your level can seriously hurt your frame rate, especially if not set up correctly. There are a few best practices when it comes to optimizing vegetation:

- Vegetation should only cast shadows where absolutely necessary
- Vegetation objects should almost always have aggressive LODs set up
- The view distance of vegetation objects should only be as far as absolutely necessary

In general, a lot of problems with the vegetation in CryENGINE are avoided by using good quality assets that have been set up properly.

Layers

The CryENGINE object layer system is an important tool when working and collaborating on a level. Another benefit of the layer system, however, is that it can be used during runtime to switch certain layers on and off. This allows you to place all your eye candy objects that are not relevant for your gameplay on a specific layer, which is only enabled when the game is run with one of the higher configuration settings. You can activate or deactivate object layers using the flowgraph at level start or later during runtime.

The Engine:LayerSwitch node allows you to turn layers on and off easily

Testing and QA

It won't be news to you that you should test your game thoroughly before shipping it out to players. As mentioned earlier, *you can only create a first impression once.*

Of course, not every developer has its own **Quality Assurance (QA)** team, which tests the build regularly throughout the development process. But even if you are a small indie developer or a Mod team, you can find testers for your game. Besides friends and family, there are thousands of forums for gamers and game developers out there where you can start looking for testers for your game. Offer rewards to testers as an additional incentive and remember to collect hardware information—every PC configuration is different. You will want to test your game on as many different systems as possible.

Steam, for example, conducts a regular survey about the hardware and software their customers are using. The data they collect includes the most common Windows versions and even the display resolutions. The information is published on their website and can be a great resource for you to gather data about the average gaming PC configuration. You can use it to decide what type of computers to test your game on.

At the very least, make sure that you test your game on at least the following systems in as many combinations as possible:

- 32-bit
- 64-bit
- NVIDIA graphics card
- ATI graphics card
- DirectX 10 GPU
- DirectX 11 GPU
- Windows 7
- Windows 8

You should always test on non-developer machines, meaning computers that do not have Visual Studio or any other development tools installed. Only then can you find out whether there is an incompatibility with older system libraries, whether you forgot to include the installer for a redistributable package, or that you accidentally shipped binaries that were compiled in debug.

While only you can decide which features of your game to test during beta testing, and how to test these, always pay special attention to the load and save functionalities. Not much will make players abandon your game faster than a broken save game.

Errors and warnings

During development, there will be a lot of errors, warnings, and other information showing up in your console and game logfile. While this is quite normal for a game under development, it should be noted that a high amount of warnings and other printouts in the console should be avoided for two reasons:

- A high amount of spam in the console can impact performance, even if not visible to the player
- Errors and warnings in the game log do not make a good impression on the player and make your game look broken, even if they are not critical

Printing errors, warnings, or other log outputs into the console and game log are expensive. A high number of so-called *log spam* can increase load time and impact the frame rate. You can find three different types of output in your game log:

- **Errors**: These appear in the console or logfile whenever the `CryLogError` functions have been used in either C++ or Lua script. All errors should be investigated and removed even if the game seems to run fine. You might potentially be shipping a bug waiting to happen when you ship your game with unresolved error logs.
- **Warnings**: These appear in the console or logfile whenever something in CryENGINE doesn't go quite as smoothly as it should and the `CryLogWarning` function was used. A warning might be caused by a missing file, a crash in a Lua script, or other events. Warnings should be investigated and fixed wherever possible. Whenever a warning cannot be resolved or turns out to be of a less critical nature, it can be removed in the code or script.
- **Logs**: Most of the time, these outputs simply provide information about an action or procedure being completed successfully. While they are usually not critical, it makes sense to have a look and see which log outputs are really needed and which have been forgotten by developers.

A common method of debugging during the development of a new feature is to output status messages to the logfile. Unfortunately, it is just as common that a coder forgets to remove these debug messages when they check the code? Search the code for leftover `CryLogAlways()` function calls to get rid of these.

Log verbosity

A quick way to deal with a high amount of log spam is to use the **log verbosity** console variable. The `log_Verbosity` console variable takes the following parameters:

- `-1`: Suppresses all logs (including `CryLogAlways()` calls)

- 0: Suppresses all logs (excluding `CryLogAlways()` calls)
- 1: Same as level 0 and additional errors are logged
- 2: Same as level 1 and additional warnings are logged
- 3: Same as level 2 and additional messages are logged
- 4: Same as level 3 and additional comments are logged

Setting the log verbosity to -1 will effectively suppress all log outputs and potentially eliminate all log spam. Although this is a pretty safe solution to remove all log spam, it is recommended that you resolve occurring errors and warnings instead of just disabling them completely. In addition to the `log_Verbosity` console variable, you can also use the `log_WriteToFileVerbosity` console variable, which will suppress anything to be written into the logfile. While this may help you in cases of extreme log spam, it also means that in the case of an error there are no logfiles you can use to investigate the actual problem.

> While disabling all log outputs solves performance problems caused by log spam, it is recommended that you investigate and fix the issues causing the log outputs instead of just suppressing the output.

Tackling legal issues

One of the worst things that can happen to you after shipping your game is getting sued because you violated someone's copyright or license terms. Even if your game is non-commercial, you are not saved from getting sued.

Copyright

Almost all copyright violations related to video games happen accidentally and are not intentionally done by developers. This, however, does not protect you from getting sued over the misstep. However, there are a few pitfalls that can be avoided to minimize the risk.

The gravity and consequences of violating a copyright depends on many factors, such as the type and IP of your game, the country you are in, your publisher, and many other things. Even if you violate someone's copyright, it doesn't automatically mean you will get sued. Maybe the owner is accommodating and won't mind. Maybe you are too small to be worth the legal trouble.

However, you should never assume that you won't get sued just because you are a small team without any money. Many large companies have very strict policies and will pursue any violations to their rights out of principle. They have to do this or they will have a hard time pursuing copyright violations from anybody else.

Although this problem is not CryENGINE-specific and copyright violations can happen no matter which engine you use, it is worth mentioning the most important points:

- Make sure you check all models, textures, and audio files. Do not ship your game with files taken from other games or web tutorials.

- Check your codebase for any third-party code used and make sure everything can be legally used in a commercial project.

- In case you are creating a commercial title, make sure you are not using any textures, sounds, animations, models, or any other asset from the CryENGINE SDK unless you have the explicit permission from Crytek. The standard FreeSDK license does not currently allow you to use the included textures and 3D models commercially. To avoid warning log spam when removing the SDK assets, you can, for example, replace all SDK textures with 4 pixel white textures of your own.

- Make sure all third party tools are licensed properly. If your commercial game was created with student or trial versions of certain programs, you might be headed for trouble.

Just as with many other things, taking care of those legal issues early during production will save you a lot of time in the end.

Credits

One of the more fun parts of preparing your game for release is the creation of the credits. How and when you display the credits to your player, and whether you go for a scrolling text or a fun video with picture and outtakes is entirely up to you. There is, however, a legal side to the credits, which you need to consider.

Credits are not only there to boost the developers' egos, they also serve a purpose in copyright. Legally speaking, almost everyone who worked on your game has a right to have their name listed in the credits, regardless of the size of his or her contribution or whether you parted ways as friends or enemies. This is the reason why a lot of AAA game credits and almost all movie credits are so very long.

You should always avoid legal conflicts wherever you can, so keep a good record of everyone who ever contributed to your game. Have a list of e-mail addresses of everyone so that you can get in touch and ask how they would like their name to appear.

Aside from the members of your team, you might need to include other third parties in your credits. Are you using someone's video plugin to play back videos in your game? Check if they require to be credited. Have you purchased models at **TurboSquid**? Are you using royalty-free music from some website? Any **Creative Commons** content? Even if you can legally use this content in your commercial game, most of the licenses require that the original creator of the content be credited. Apart from the legal issues, you are using someone else's work and giving them credit for it should be a matter of honor. Keep a list of every asset you purchased and imported in your game and make sure that you include everybody in your credits.

CryENGINE license

Very often during the development of a game, the scope and size of a game might change. Maybe you switched from a mod to a full standalone game. Maybe your noncommercial project turned out even better than you hoped and you are considering putting your game on Steam. Or maybe you hit it big on Steam and now want to press your game on DVD and bring it into **Target** and **GameStop**.

Each of these scenarios will require a different license. Before you put your game out on the market, be sure that you have acquired the proper license from Crytek.

 At the time of writing, the Free SDK license does not allow any kind of commercial use of CryENGINE. The indie license is only valid for digital distribution platforms. License terms are subject to change, of course. Always read the license agreement before shipping your build.

Things to consider for indies

When you are working on a commercial indie game with a small team of people, it is important to have every team member sign a release agreement and proper contract for their work on the game. A team member who worked on your game *for free* might later come back to sue you, even if you verbally agreed that the work was done for free.

Another issue that happens far too often occurs when a team member leaves the project and declares that their code/music/graphics/models/whatever can no longer be used in the game, because they want to use them in a different project.

It is not uncommon for indie or mod teams to give out mandatory NDAs and release forms. You don't want to have to bin your project after a year of worked weekends and nights because your 3D artists have decided to give the rights to your hero character to another project.

Make sure you always set up the proper paperwork and have everybody on your team sign it. As *corporate* as that may sound, it protects the hard work and time of everyone else in the team.

MobyGames

MobyGames is a large database that collects information about published games. It catalogs things such as the release year, publisher, and developer, and allows users to vote and rank the games. You should consider adding your game here and supply them with your credits list.

The reason you should add your game is not primarily to get a great user ranking for it. There are other game review sites that will be more important when promoting your game. MobyGames will, however, create an entry in their database for each one of your team members.

This can become very important as this site is often checked by developers when they receive job applications. The name of the applicant is put into the search function of the site and a list of all projects he/she has worked on will be displayed. This can go a long way in terms of credibility and is an easy way for you to help your team members out.

Preparing your build

There are several steps to get your build ready to be shipped. These involve the removal of source files and packing up the game's data into PAK files. Depending on your project, you might need additional steps.

The main executable of CryENGINE is sometimes called `Launcher.exe` and sometimes `GameSDK.exe`, depending on the SDK version. To avoid confusion, this chapter will refer to the file as `Launcher.exe`.

Building a release candidate

It should go without saying that you should not simply take the build from one of your coder's machines and ship it. To prepare your build for shipping, you will need to do more than just compile the code.

- Compile source code
  - This needs to be done for 32-bit and 64-bit solution configurations.
  - Make sure the code is not compiled in debug; coders forget this more often than they care to admit. The code should be compiled in *release*.

- Compile assets
- Export all levels
  - Only then can they be loaded in the Launcher

- Rename `Launcher.exe`
  - This is your game's main executable file and you might want to rename the file to the name of your game. This has to be done in both the `Bin32` and `Bin64` folders. This step is optional, of course.

- Convert WAV files to MP2
  - This step is optional and only applies if you are using these files directly instead of using FMOD. The lame encoder can be found in the CryENGINE tools directory.

Hopefully, you have set up a version control for your project and put a build server in place. In that case, you are already well prepared to ship your game, as your build scripts will already compile your code, process your assets, and pack them into PAK files. If you haven't, now is the time to head back to *Chapter 1, Setting Up the Perfect Pipeline*.

Auto-loading the first level

When your players start the game, they need to be taken to the main menu or your first level automatically. By default, the CryENGINE **Launcher** does not load a level. If you need this functionality, you can use the `autoexec` config file to specify a start level to load whenever the Launcher is started.

Simply create a text file called `autoexec.cfg` in the CryENGINE root folder. Edit it in Notepad or a text editing program of your choice and add the following content:

```
map Name_Of_Your_First_Level
```

PAK files

When it is time to ship your game, you should make sure that all content files belonging to your game are packed up in PAK files, CryENGINE's proprietary archive file format. Shipping PAK files has several advantages. PAK files can, for example, be encrypted to prevent players from looking at the game files. You will most likely not want players messing with your game's data files. This is not primarily to prevent cheating or modding—the latter might even be welcomed—but because most users will not know what they are doing. The chances of your game's data becoming corrupt are high when you allow free access to your files.

Another reason to pack your game data into PAK files is to offer an easy way to repair broken games for your users. You can simply compare file sizes or checksums of a handful of PAK files and have them redownloaded or reinstalled, than check the tens of thousands of individual files that belong to your installation.

Fast-loading PAK files

In addition to being easier to handle, PAK files can also be used to load certain content ahead of your bulk data. When your game starts, there will be certain assets that are required earlier than others. These might, for example, include models and textures used in your main menu.

To avoid stalls and load time at game start, certain assets can be packed up and loaded right away before anything else. This so-called *fast loading* can be set up easily. You can find a folder called *FastLoad* in the root of the CryENGINE SDK (GameSDK by default). Each PAK file located in this folder will be loaded on priority and be available right away at game start. Only files used very often and early in your game should be contained inside those PAK files.

In addition to the PAK files located inside the `FastLoad` folder, level-specific files can also be cached to improve the performance of your levels. The `LevelCache` folder located inside the root of your projects game folder can hold multiple PAK files for individual levels.

▸ Builds ▸ CRYENGINE_PC_v_3_5_3_FreeSDK ▸ GameSDK ▸ _LevelCache ▸ Singleplayer ▸ Forest

Name	Date modified	Type	Size
cga.pak	8/23/2013 7:06 AM	PAK File	86 KB
cgf.pak	8/23/2013 7:06 AM	PAK File	17,946 KB
chr.pak	8/23/2013 7:06 AM	PAK File	683 KB
skin.pak	8/23/2013 7:06 AM	PAK File	2,368 KB
xml.pak	8/23/2013 7:06 AM	PAK File	832 KB

Level-specific cache files are stored inside the `_LevelCache` folder

All of the commonly used assets can be stored inside those PAK files and used to speed up level performance. Each of the files in this folder holds specific assets used in the particular level, such as `.cga`, `.cgf`, and `.chr` files. Although those PAK files can be built manually, it is recommended to automate this process. CryENGINE can automatically generate a list of the resources used in a level, which can then be used to create level cache PAK files. To automatically create level cache files, follow these steps:

1. Set the console variable `sys_PakSaveLevelResourceList` to 1 in the `system.cfg` file. This will automatically create resource lists for you.

2. Start your game in Launcher and not in Sandbox, and load a level.

This will create a resource called the `auto_resourcelist.txt` list file inside your level folder. A list of all the files that should be loaded early on is stored in this file. You can create resource list files for every level, by performing the preceding steps. The resource list files will become important during the build process. The resource compiler folder, usually located in your SDK root folder in `../Bin32/rc/..`, contains a file called `RCJob_PerLevelCache_SDK.xml`. Within this file, the level-specific resource lists are used to generate PAK files for each level.

Removing all debug features

This one should be considered carefully. During the development of your project, you will likely implement several methods to debug your various game systems.

On one hand, you want to remove these debugging features so that players don't accidentally hit a debug key on the keyboard and get bombarded with lines and arrows in their rendering. Or worse, they find the cheat key to instantly kill the final boss in your level, get unlimited gold, or fly around.

On the other hand, you can never be 100 percent certain that your game will be absolutely bug free. And when those bug reports come flooding into your forum, you might be glad to be able to ask your players for some debug screenshots or logfiles with the debug output.

In a nutshell, you need to decide which debug features you want to disable and which ones you want to leave in. By default, you should at least disable all debug keys. If you want, you can set up a CVar to re-enable them, so that your players can provide you with valuable debug info. If you have grouped all your debug keys into a debug Action Map as recommended in *Chapter 2, Using the CryENGINE Input System – Keyboard, Mouse, and Game Controller*, you can simply prevent the loading of this map with a CVar.

```
pDebugActionMap->SetActionListener( actorId );
```

As CryENGINE is an openly available engine, its debug features are publicly known and documented as well. You might, for example, disable the key that opens the console or map it to a different key to make messing around with your game at least a little harder.

Reducing your build size

By the time you are ready to ship your game, your CryENGINE build will be quite large. Most likely, the number of files you ship will be in the thousands. With all the source files, you can easily have a total size of 20, 50, or even 100 GB. In order to keep the build as small and lean as possible, it is important to remove all unnecessary files from the build before shipping. In addition to reducing the build size, you don't want to ship the source files to your textures and models to your players.

There are many ways to automatically remove these unneeded files as part of your build process. The build scripts included in this book include a step that filters out files based on their file type or filename. You will likely have a number of files in your project that you don't want to ship, but want to keep in your version control system. You can add them to the filter list to have them automatically removed. See the *Automated builds and build scripts* section in *Chapter 1, Setting Up the Perfect Pipeline* for details.

There are a number of files you should remove from the build before giving it out to others to play in addition to the ones filtered out by the build process. These are files that you want to keep in your internal builds, like the Sandbox Editor, for example, but don't want your players to have access to.

Files you should not ship are:

- All kinds of source files, such as .psd, .max, and .tif
    - The build scripts should already take care of this

- Old files and files not used anymore
- Source files to shaders
    - As the FreeSDK does not include the source files to the shaders, this is usually not relevant to indie developers

- Source files to your levels
    - Remove the *.cry files from your build. Otherwise, your players will be able to edit your levels and cheat or steal your data.

- Tools and exporters
    - The exporters for Max, Maya, and so on are not needed to play your game. You can remove these from your `Tools` folder.
    - According to the official documentation, you can even remove the entire `Tools` folder when shipping your game. However, there have been issues reported with this, so be sure to test this thoroughly.

- Sandbox Editor
    - Remove `Editor.exe` or `Sandbox.exe` from your `Bin32` and `Bin64` folders

- Editor folder
    - This folder is located in your CryENGINE root directory. It contains only files that are needed by the Sandbox Editor. These don't need to be distributed with your game.

- Source code
    - You can remove the entire `Code` folder. If you are using the build scripts to pack your code into a ZIP file, make sure not to ship this out to your customers.

- Example and reference files, and test levels
    - Level designers like to use reference images when building terrain, coders use test levels to develop their features in, and artists might create example models to test setups. These files are sometimes extremely large and have no purpose in your final game.

Shaders

The CryENGINE shader system is based on the HLSL shader language. All materials in a CryENGINE environment will use a more or less complex shader. Each material using the same shader will probably use different parameters to customize it. This creates so-called **shader permutations**, with each permutation being a different variation of the same base shader. Compiling these shader permutations takes quite a bit of time and should not be done at runtime. This is why it is important to ship your game with an up-to-date shader cache, which already includes all permutations needed. The `Engine` folder in your CryENGINE root directory holds the PAK files that contain the shader cache.

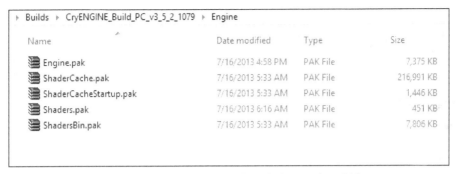

Name	Date modified	Type	Size
Engine.pak	7/16/2013 4:58 PM	PAK File	7,375 KB
ShaderCache.pak	7/16/2013 5:33 AM	PAK File	216,991 KB
ShaderCacheStartup.pak	7/16/2013 5:33 AM	PAK File	1,446 KB
Shaders.pak	7/16/2013 6:16 AM	PAK File	451 KB
ShadersBin.pak	7/16/2013 5:33 AM	PAK File	7,806 KB

The compiled shaders are located inside the `Engine` folder

Shipping your game with an up-to-date shader cache makes sure that the players will not have to wait for shaders being compiled as a level is being started.

Whenever CryENGINE renders an object for the first time, it will check if the shaders used in its materials have been compiled already. In case a precompiled shader is not available, it will try and look it up in the shader cache. In this way, shader permutations can be looked up quickly. If there is no compiled shader found, however, the engine will compile the shader at runtime. Obviously, this should be avoided since it causes stalls and visual artifacts during runtime.

Your game will not look pretty if the shaders are uncompiled

When being generated, the shader cache is placed into the `User/Shaders` folder inside your CryENGINE root directory.

Before shipping your game, make sure you have an up-to-date shader cache PAK file to avoid stalls and visual problems caused by shaders being compiled at runtime.

More information on the general functionality of the CryENGINE shader system and additional information on the process of automatically creating the shader cache PAK files can be found in the official CryENGINE documentation.

Creating an installer

As much as CryENGINE demands a certain level of technical expertise from you, the developer, to create a game, you cannot expect your customers to read through long manuals or documentation after they downloaded your game. They will want to double-click on your game's icon and start playing. It is your job to make this as easy for them as possible.

A ZIP file

You can choose to simply pack your build up into a ZIP file and distribute a download link. Any modern Windows system can open ZIP files without any additional software, and the creation is free.

 Before you decide to ship your build using this method, make sure to read the section about dependencies. Your players might need to manually download and install additional packages before they can play your game.

If you choose the ZIP file method, keep in mind that your customers still need an easy way to start your game. You won't have the luxury of automatic shortcut creation on the desktop or in the start menu. To run your game, your users will need to navigate to either the `Bin32` or `Bin64` folder, locate the `Launcher.exe` file (or whatever you renamed the file to), and start it.

You can ease their way by creating a simple BAT file in your game's base folder that will autodetect whether it is running on a 32- or 64-bit system, start the correct file, and launch it.

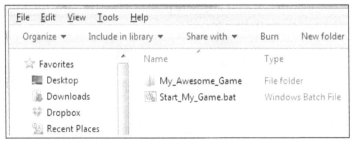

Your users will appreciate a simple way to start your game

The following code will query the registry and then start the correct executable. This is just a sample; you can of course also create this functionality in a variety of different ways.

```
@echo off

Set RegQry=HKLM\Hardware\Description\System\CentralProcessor\0

REG.exe Query %RegQry% > checkOS.txt

Find /i "x86" < CheckOS.txt > StringCheck.txt

If %ERRORLEVEL% == 0 (
    REM Echo "This is 32 Bit Operating system"
  del CheckOS.txt
  del StringCheck.txt
  .\My_Awesome_Game\Bin32\Launcher.exe
) ELSE (
    REM Echo "This is 64 Bit Operating System"
  del CheckOS.txt
  del StringCheck.txt
  .\My_Awesome_Game\Bin64\Launcher.exe
)
```

Selecting an installer

Creating an installer for your game means packing up into an executable file, which your players can download. It will start an installation wizard and guide your player through a couple of steps to install your game in the right directory. It can create shortcuts for it on the desktop and in the start menu, and link them to the correct versions of your launcher executable. A good installer can install additional dependencies as well as write uninstall information to the registry. This allows your players to comfortably remove your game from their system again.

You don't have to write this installer by yourself, as there are multiple software packages available that offer this functionality already. Some cost money and offer more features, while others are available for free.

Sophisticated installer creation tools are, for example, InstallShield Express, InstallAware, and Nullsoft NSIS. InstallAware offers a free version and NSIS is completely free and can be used for commercial purposes. Select the installer of your choice based on your preferences and available funding. Your overall build size might also become important, as some installers don't support large-sized builds.

The simplest way to create the most basic of installers is to use the iExpress tool that comes preinstalled on most Windows operating systems. Note that there is no start menu entry for it; you will need to type `iexpress.exe` into the command line in the start menu.

This tool will essentially only create a self-extracting executable file for you. It can let your player choose where to install your game and display a license, but it won't create any shortcuts, put uninstall information in the registry, or install additional dependencies.

> To save hard disk space, you might not want to install/extract both the `Bin32` and `Bin64` directories, as each of these is about 150 MB in size. Keep in mind that you should always install the `Bin32/RC` subfolder, however, so that the resource compiler is available.

Dependencies

Regardless of whether you packed your build into a ZIP file or created a custom installer, simply giving out the CryENGINE build won't be enough to allow your customers to play your game. Your players will need to have some additional packages installed.

CryENGINE requires the **DirectX End-User Runtime** to be installed, as well as the redistributables packages for Visual Studio. As these are redistributables, you can include them in your download package and even make them a part of your installer.

Apart from CryENGINE, you might be making use of other third-party software, which has its own requirements. A common dependency is the Windows SDK redistributables, for example. If you tested your build thoroughly on clean machines before release, you will already have a list of the required packages.

> Be sure to check the official documentation for the latest list of dependencies, as this is sometimes updated with new CryENGINE releases.

An icon for your executable

When you ship your game, obviously you will want your executable file to have your game's icon. You will also want this icon to be used in the desktop shortcut and in the start menu entry.

You will need to create your icon in multiple sizes. CryENGINE ships with an icon in three sizes: 128 x 128, 256 x 256, and 512 x 512. More common sizes are 64 x 64 and 32 x 32. If you don't supply an icon in a specific resolution, Windows will simply scale it. While downscaling icons are usually no problem, upscaling a 64 x 64 icon to 128 x 128 will rarely look good.

You can exchange the icon for the CryENGINE executable file in the **Resource View** in Visual Studio. The icon can be found in the **PCLauncher** project, in `launcher.rc`. You will need to recompile the Launcher after you exchange the icon.

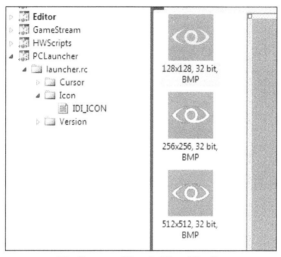

The Resource View in Visual Studio

The preceding method of exchanging the icon is not available to Free SDK users, as it requires access to the full source code of CryENGINE. If you don't have a license that includes the source to the Launcher project, you can use a third-party tool such as *Resource Hacker* to change the icon on the executable.

Summary

In this chapter, all the important aspects of getting a CryENGINE game ready to ship were discussed. Which files were contained in a build and which ones should not be shipped, as well as performance issues which might make an impact on your game were also explained. The information provided in this chapter should help you to get your game to a stable and clean state, so that it can be released to the general public.

This was the final chapter of *Mastering CryENGINE*. We, the authors, hope you learned a lot about CryENGINE and how it can be used to create great game content. Now, it is up to you to put your knowledge and creativity to good use and build a great CryENGINE game.

Index

B

beautification passes **225**
Beyond Compare **23**
binaries **16**
bug
  about **39**
  tracking, software **39**
buildbot **19**
BuildBotPath **22**
BuildLog.txt **29**
builds
  assets, compiling **25-29**
  automated builds, scheduling **30-33**
  build size, reducing **241, 242**
  code, compiling **24, 25, 238**
  custom build script, creating **19, 20**
  debug features, removing **240**
  first level, auto loading **238**
  latest files, getting **22-24**
  nightly builds, creating **17**
  operating systems **18**
  own script, writing **20-22**
  PAK files, shipping **239**
  preparing **237**
  scripts **18**
  server, setting up **17**
  shaders **242-244**
build script
  custom build script, creating **19, 20**
  own script, writing **20-22**
build server
  setting up **17**
build size
  reducing **241, 242**
BuildSourcePath **22**
BuildTargetPath **22**
BuildWithLogFile.bat **29**
BuildWorkPath **22**

C

C++
  used, for creating nodes **94**
camera
  camera target, manipulating **128, 129**
  switching **129**
  working with **127**

camera tag-points
  using **124, 125**
camera target
  manipulating **128, 129**
characters head
  exporting, for facial setup **96, 97**
Client/Server function **147, 148**
code
  compiling, for build **238**
coding
  for animation **180, 181**
commercial indie game
  legal issues **236**
  MobyGames **237**
component node **77, 78**
console commands
  triggering **57**
copyright **234**
credits **235**
CryENGINE
  animation system **159, 160**
  issue tracking **40**
  Lua script, utilizing in **135, 136**
  new version, integrating **36-38**
  performance tests **34**
CryENGINE 2.0 **75**
CryENGINE 3 **159**
CryENGINE 3.5 **160**
CryENGINE game
  errors **233**
  layers, optimizing **231**
  legal issues, tackling **234**
  level, optimizing **228**
  performance, optimizing **228**
  shadows, optimizing **229, 230**
  testing **232**
  vegetation, optimizing **231**
  warnings **233**
CryENGINE license **236**
CryENGINE projects
  excluded files, identifying **16**
  production pipeline **7, 8**
  VCS **8**
  VCS, selecting for **10**
CryENGINE Sandbox
  about **117**
  custom commands, exploring **129, 130**

vegetation, CryENGINE game
  optimizing 231
version control system. *See* VCS
video recording 131
visimes
  creating, for lip sync quality 115
Visual Studio 14, 15

X

Xbox 360 controller
  Input event name 72

Z

zip file 244, 245

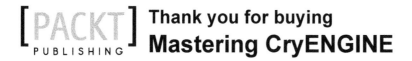
Thank you for buying
Mastering CryENGINE

About Packt Publishing

Packt, pronounced 'packed', published its first book "*Mastering phpMyAdmin for Effective MySQL Management*" in April 2004 and subsequently continued to specialize in publishing highly focused books on specific technologies and solutions.

Our books and publications share the experiences of your fellow IT professionals in adapting and customizing today's systems, applications, and frameworks. Our solution based books give you the knowledge and power to customize the software and technologies you're using to get the job done. Packt books are more specific and less general than the IT books you have seen in the past. Our unique business model allows us to bring you more focused information, giving you more of what you need to know, and less of what you don't.

Packt is a modern, yet unique publishing company, which focuses on producing quality, cutting-edge books for communities of developers, administrators, and newbies alike. For more information, please visit our website: www.packtpub.com.

Writing for Packt

We welcome all inquiries from people who are interested in authoring. Book proposals should be sent to author@packtpub.com. If your book idea is still at an early stage and you would like to discuss it first before writing a formal book proposal, contact us; one of our commissioning editors will get in touch with you.

We're not just looking for published authors; if you have strong technical skills but no writing experience, our experienced editors can help you develop a writing career, or simply get some additional reward for your expertise.

CryENGINE Game Programming with C++, C#, and Lua

ISBN: 978-1-84969-590-9   Paperback: 276 pages

Get to grips with the essential tools for developing games with the awesome and powerful CryENGINE

1. Dive into the various CryENGINE subsystems to quickly learn how to master the engine.

2. Create your very own game using C++, C#, or Lua in CryENGINE.

3. Understand the structure and design of the engine.

CryENGINE 3 Game Development: Beginner's Guide

ISBN: 978-1-84969-200-7   Paperback: 354 pages

Discover how to use the CryENGINE 3 free SDK, the next-generation, real-time game development tool

1. Begin developing your own games of any scale by learning to harness the power of the Award Winning CryENGINE® 3 game engine.

2. Build your game worlds in real-time with CryENGINE® 3 Sandbox as we share insights into some of the tools and features useable right out of the box.

3. Harness your imagination by learning how to create customized content for use within your own custom games through the detailed asset creation examples within the book.

Please check **www.PacktPub.com** for information on our titles

Slick2D Game Development

ISBN: 978-1-78328-983-7   Paperback: 116 pages

Develop simple, yet engaging games with the Slick2D game engine

1. Work with Slick2D game workflow.

2. Learn how to develop game components with hands-on examples.

3. Get to grips with game analysis and enhancement.

Unity 4.x Game Development by Example: Beginner's Guide

ISBN: 978-1-84969-526-8   Paperback: 572 pages

A seat-of-your-pants manual for building fun, groovy little games quickly with Unity 4.x

1. Learn the basics of the Unity 3D game engine by building five small, functional game projects.

2. Explore simplification and iteration techniques that will make you more successful as a game developer.

3. Take Unity for a spin with a refreshingly humorous approach to technical manuals.

Please check **www.PacktPub.com** for information on our titles

www.ingramcontent.com/pod-product-compliance
Lightning Source LLC
Chambersburg PA
CBHW060528060326
40690CB00017B/3422